THE KENTUCKY REVIVAL, OR, A SHORT HISTORY

OF THE LATE EXTRAORDINARY OUT-POURING OF THE SPIRIT OF GOD, IN THE WESTERN STATES OF AMERICA, AGREEABLY TO SCRIPTURE PROMISES, AND PROPHECIES CONCERNING THE LATTER DAY:

WITH A BRIEF ACCOUNT
OF THE ENTRANCE AND PROGRESS OF WHAT THE WORLD CALL
SHAKERISM,
AMONG THE SUBJECTS OF THE LATE REVIVAL IN *OHIO* AND *KENTUCKY*.
PRESENTED TO THE
TRUE ZION-TRAVELLER,
AS A MEMORIAL OF THE WILDERNESS JOURNEY.

BY RICHARD MCNEMAR.

"When ye see a cloud rise out of the west, straightway ye say,
"there cometh a shower ; and so it is: And when YE FEEL
"the south wind blow, ye say, there will be heat ; and it
"cometh to pass, Can ye not discern the signs of the times."

CHRIST.

1808.

This updated edition copyright 2012 by Michael D. Fortner, all rights reserved.

Softcover trade paperback:

ISBN-978-0-9982172-3-9

Originally published in 1808.

Trumpet Press is a member of the Christian Small Publisher's Association (CSPA)

Table of Contents

A letter 5
To the Reader 7
Chapter One 9
Chapter Two.. 19
Chapter Three.. 29
Chapter Four 41

Shakerism
Among the Subjects of the Late Revival

Chapter One 73
Chapter Two.. 87
A few reflections.. 105
Appendix... 111

New Things — New Names

The word SHAKERISM, I never saw until it appeared in a pamphlet published in Kentucky, a few years ago, in defense of what is called the *schismatic* doctrine (see Stone's Reply, p. 66). I suppose it is derived from *shaker*, one who shakes; in the same manner that *schismatism* springs from *schismatic*, i.e. one who divides or separates from the church.

Preface to the Modern Edition

The information in this book is very enlightening for many reasons. One of the reasons these early camp-meetings have not received the attention they deserve is because unusual manifestations of the Spirit were seen throughout, not just in a few places, or for a few years. It was opposition to these manifestations that ultimately brought the Second Great Awakening to a close, as seen in other books.

This first appearance in print of the term "*Holy Roller*" was actually in the early 1800s, which means it was likely the result of this revival, and not early Pentecostalism, as often believed.

This one was written in 1807 and this edition printed in 1808.

I have edited this book to update it to modern English; I changed the spelling of words like "pow'rs" to "powers" and changed a few words we no longer use to the modern equivalent, while other words I have given the meaning in brackets [**]. I have also improved the punctuation slightly, but I have done NO rewriting; only editing. The original page numbers, corresponding to the page numbers on the 1808 edition at the top of each page, are included in brackets, such as [1]. So the text below it was on page 1.

Read, and be amazed,
Michael D. Fortner

[3]
A LETTER

From the Author, to a friend in New-Lebanon, State of *New-York,* accompanying the *Kentucky Revival.*

THESE few lines will accompany a little Book entitled the *Kentucky Revival,* which on account of many singularities, cannot be so well understood at a distance from this place. I shall therefore suggest a few considerations, which may be proper for any who may think this little history worth their perusal.

I. The people for whose information it was written, are singular from all others on the face of the earth, principally, on account of the very extraordinary and singular work of God, which of late years, has been wrought among them; by reason of which, so great a diversity of sentiments have sprung up, and such different degrees of light been attained.

II. Too great a majority of the subjects of this mighty work, through the subtlety of Satan, and the influence of prejudice and false reports, have shut their eyes against the pure light of the Gospel for which they sat out, and were eventually so remarkably prepared; and contrary to all which they had been taught by the spirit of truth, declined any further search for the kingdom, and set to build themselves up on what they had received. Therefore it appeared as though it would be fruitless labor, to go to writing about the Gospel, and opening the way of salvation to such, while they conceived that they had already attained to that which would answer their purpose.

The first labor then, was to go over this old ground, and show, according to their own sense, what that work had affected. And here a foreigner can have but little understanding of those debates about doctrines, bodily [4] exercises, gifts of the spirit, signs, etc. which are so fresh on the memories of the generality in this country.

III. Many allusions are made to other writings extant in this country; such as *The Apology, Stone's letters on Atonement, Reply, Address to the different Religious Societies, Western Calender, etc.* [sic] without which many expressions, figures and particular modes of reasoning, must be wholly obscure.

IV. It appears remarkable, that if anything can benefit those who have pitched their tents short of mount Zion, it must be a faithful account of their former journey by one who travelled with them, step by step, with a plain investigation of the paths into which they were finally led by the adversary of all righteousness.

When things are stated just as they took place, from the first rays of light that stirred up the people to see the blackness of antichrist's kingdom, until the true Gospel and church of Christ was revealed; it then remains for each to judge for himself, whether he is in possession of that which cannot be shaken.

RICHARD MCNEMAR,
Turtle Creek, September 13, 1807

Chapter 1

[5]
TO THE READER

YOU have been probably waiting for something to be published from this quarter, may be a little surprised to find the *Kentucky Revival* our theme; as it is generally known that we profess to have advanced forward into a much greater work.

Admitting this to be the case (which we do not deny) it would nevertheless be improper to forget, or set light by any operation or work of the true spirit, however small it might seem. But far from esteeming the Kentucky Revival a day of small things, we believe it was nothing less than an *introduction* to that work of *final redemption,* which God had promised in the latter days. And to preserve the memory of it among those who have wisely improved it as such, the following particulars have been collected for the press, by one, whose spirit was in it from the beginning, and who is a living witness of the most important particulars which occurred in every stage of it, until the present day.

For the better understanding of the following history, it will be proper to make a few preliminary observations.

It will be granted, that God has a particular order and manner of working, in which one thing goes before another. Thus: *the law and the prophets were until John,* after that *the kingdom of heaven is preached.* It then follows that *all men press into it.* The first thing is the *law,* which convinces of sin. 2. The *Prophets* who minister the promise and hope of salvation. 3. The *kingdom of heaven is preached;* the way and method of salvation made manifest in word and doctrine: and last of all we must *press into it.* This is the order of

God, and there is no other. Nothing short of pressing into the kingdom can save the soul. Conviction may die away; hope and comfort desert the breast; and the [6] most lively views of the kingdom be forgotten. Hence the necessity of so often reviving these things among professors. But whatever can die away, is short of the kingdom of God; those who are in the kingdom have everlasting life. Therefore it is plain that the constituent parts of a revival (which are conviction of sin, a hope of deliverance from it, and a manifestation of the *heavenly state*) can only be preparative to entering into it. How many revivals have taken place in these latter days, which for a season would raise the people, as it were, to heaven's gate; and after all, leave them to fall back into their former listless state. And why so? Because they did not take the last step, and press into that state which in word and doctrine was opened.

II. It will be granted, that whoever preaches the kingdom of heaven, must preach deliverance from all sin: For where sin is, there can be no heaven. Now when the kingdom has been preached, and honest souls have fixed their eye of faith upon it, longed with intense desire to be in it, and solicitously enquired for the footsteps of those who have already entered: then has been the time for the grand deceiver to come in with his doctrine of procrastination, and preach up sin for term of life; appeal to the doleful experience of past generations, and confirm the fatal error by the doctrines and decrees of a corrupt church. Thus the most promising revivals have been blasted, and all that near sense of heaven's pure enjoyments (common under the preaching of the kingdom) extinguished by men of corrupt minds.

But the *Kentucky Revival,* from the beginning, spoke better things. Those who were the genuine subjects of it, ever expressed the fullest confidence that it would not terminate as revivals had generally done. It was not a common portion of law conviction; nor that faith in the promise, which put heaven at a distance; nor merely preaching about the kingdom that drew out the multitudes to encamp for days and nights in the wilderness, etc. It was a near prospect of the true [7] kingdom of God, into which many were determined to press at the expense of all that they held dear upon earth. The late revival was not sent to RE-FORM the churches. It did not come with a piece of new cloth to patch the old garment, to mend up the old hope with some new experience; but to prepare the way for that kingdom of God, in which all things are new: and whether it be in many or few, the purposes whereunto it was sent, undoubtedly be answered.

III. That this extraordinary work sprung from some supernatural cause has been universally granted; but whether the cause was good or evil, has been a matter of much debate, even among those who profess to take the scripture for their only guide. Christians so called, of all others have been the most divided in their judgment concerning it; and while some without hesitation have pronounced it a glorious work of God; others who professed to be children of the same father, followers of the same Savior, and instructed by the same word of God, have with equal confidence pronounced it *witchcraft, enthusiasm, fanaticism,* and *the very energy of delusion.* Hence the various predictions concerning it: Some affirming that it would shortly terminate and leave the unhappy subjects of it, in a worse condition than ever; others that it should *cover the earth, as the waters cover the sea,* and gather the nations into one united body.

IV. As the continuance of the revival was so strongly predicted and asserted by all its subjects, it will be proper to consider how far and upon what footing, those predictions and assertions are tenable. That it should always continue in the same measure and appearance without any increase, was never intended; therefore if that same power continues to work, though it should be in greater degree and more extraordinary manner, and though it should be among a different people, this will not prove the above predictions false, provided it be the same power working to the same end.

While the extraordinary power of the revival was foreign; while irresistible beams of light [8] presented objects to the view which persons could not avoid seeing, and they were rushed into exercises of body by a force of operation which they could not withstand, the continuance of the work in this fashion, was precarious, knowing that God will not always work upon man like a machine. Therefore in order to the continuance of the work, a number of its subjects have found it necessary to receive this extraordinary power as an in-dwelling treasure, to unite with this supernatural agent, to dwell in him and he in them, and become workers together with him, and without force or violence, believe and practice whatever he teaches. And on this pivot the revival turns with each individual. The power or light of God, continues with those who continue in it, his spirit abides only with those who abide in him, and do continually the things that please him; of course such as are willing that Christ and Belial should have day about [sic], light and darkness alternately prevail, must fall off and wither; for no man can serve two masters.

V. Since the spirit and the power of the revival has been established upon the above principles, and the divine agent has found a habitation with men, less attention has been paid to former appearances. This new and strange doctrine of receiving Christ, and walking in him, has engrossed the general concern: and while the singular manner of worship, strange bodily exercises. etc. of those who stand in it, have furnished matter of speculation to the world around, their distinguishing faith has been a matter of serious enquiry with many; especially those who have begun to open their eyes on the hidden glories of the kingdom of Christ, and are beginning to move Zion-ward. But before the *temple of God*

can be opened in heaven and the ark of his testament seen, it will be proper to recognize the various operations by which the materials of the *tabernacle* were prepared: According as it is written, *"Behold I send my messenger, and he shall prepare the way before me: and the Lord whom ye seek, shall suddenly come to his temple."*
  R. M.
Turtle-Creek, June 20, 1807.

[9]
Chapter One

Of the state of religion in this western country before the Kentucky Revival made its appearance.
Original Pages 9-19

In the first settlement of this country, no small part of the inhabitants were Christians by profession. Different denominations early began to shine out, and employ their zeal in organizing churches, settling ministers and propagating their respective doctrines and forms of worship throughout the land. The greatest number of professors might be ranked among the *Presbyterians, Baptists* and *Methodists*. And although these different sects professedly set out to establish and promote the peaceable religion of Jesus; yet in the attempt, their usual debates and controversies were brought to life, which, for a number of years occasioned a hot spiritual war. Notwithstanding, these churches acknowledged each other as sisters, descended from the same stock; yet such was the zeal of each for their distinguishing tenets and forms of worship, that they stood entirely separate as to any communion or fellowship, and treated each other with the highest marks of hostility; wounding, captivating, and bickering one another, until their attention was called off by the appearance of a common enemy, viz. Deism, or the religion of nature.

II. For many ages the Christian religion, so called, had been incorporated with civil government, and they had mutually supported each other, consequently when [10] that revolution in politics began, which aimed at the overthrow of the monarchy and the establishment of a republican government, *that religion* was particularly involved.

Kings, Emperors and Popes, had claimed the Bible, as "*the only rule to direct them,*" in their unnatural wars, dire oppressions, bloody persecutions, and unparalleled cruelties toward mankind; yea, every class of tyrants, both civil and ecclesiastical, had made their common appeal to the Bible, for their authority to lord it over their fellow-creatures, consequently when the eye of reason began to open upon the *rights of man,* the tyrants *Canon* must appear in very pernicious colors, no book in the universe so mischievous and hateful. And under this view the Bible was attacked by the political reformers of the last century; and the dictates of a lawless nature cried up in opposition to its sacred requirements.

III. I do not suppose with many, that Deists have had no cause for rejecting the scriptures; the contrary is certainly true. Not that the cause is in the scriptures, but in those who profess to take them for their rule of life. It is not the scriptures that lie open to the view of the Deist, but those churches and people who profess to be governed and influenced by them. And what have those churches exhibited which for ages past have claimed the Bible for their foundation? Little else but division, animosity and confusion. What have been the lives and manners of the professors in general? Do they not stand below the modern Deist, even in point of bible virtue? Now if Christians so called, are chargeable with so great wickedness, in the eye of common sense and reason, and at the same time testify that the Bible is their "*only rule,*" what judgment can the Deist form of that book? The tree is known by its fruit; and if professing Christians acknowledge themselves to be wicked, if they judge and prove one another to be wicked, and claim the *Bible* as their root and foundation; it is reasonable for the Deist to judge *that* to be a wicked book. [11]

IV. When Deism first began to overspread Kentucky; and the truth of the Bible to be called in question; the cry was against *its* pernicious fruits and the infinite mischief that has been done in the world by those who supported its doctrines. And while the giddy and thoughtless multitude took it for granted that divine revelation was all a cheat, and nature's flowery path the only way to happiness, and were crowding into it by hundreds, many of a more serious cast were unwilling to renounce their hope of salvation through Christ; yet dare not vindicate the lives of those professing Christians, on whose account the Bible was condemned. This made it necessary to examine the scriptures separately and judge them according to their internal evidence, and the more they were examined, the greater the contrast appeared between their sacred doctrines and the lives of the professors. Hence the only ground upon which the truth of the scriptures could be maintained, was to take them according to their own proper sense, and prove that they nowhere countenanced those evils that abounded in the churches; but the contrary.

V. The New Testament appeared to be the proper fruit and product of the church of Christ, and manifested by its purity, that it was a pure church out of which it sprung. And taking the church as the tree, and the scripture as the fruit, both seemed to be good. But the fruit, which has been for many generations produced by those churches which bore the same name, was very different. The writings of these churches instead of uniting the people in righteousness and peace, had kindled up endless controversies and angry disputes; and from the manifest difference in the fruits, it appeared that modern professors [of Christianity] could not be the same kind of people with those that had formerly been called Christian. According to the scriptures, Christians were united all of one heart and one soul; they laid aside all anger, wrath, clamor, envy and evil speaking; were kindly affectioned one towards another, and loved one another with pure heart fervently. But daily [12] observation proved, that those who now assumed the same name, were full of envy and strife, railing and backbiting, hateful and hating one another; and in every sense different from those holy men of God, who were formerly called by the name of Christ.

VI. This distinction was observed not only in common professors, but even in the ministers. While the New Testament represented the ministers of Christ, as meek, humble, honest men; examples to the flock, in charity, faith and purity. Those who are called the ministers of Christ in the present day, appeared to be proud, aspiring, contentious men, striving who should be the greatest, overlooking common people as an inferior rank of beings, deeply immersed in the cares of the world, eager after salaries, or posts of profit in civil government, and some even holding their fellow-creatures in perpetual slavery, or selling them for money. These appeared not to be the same kind of men as those whom Christ ordained, nor did it appear that they had the same Holy Ghost indwelling in them, or could be as safely believed or followed, as the ministers who wrote the scriptures. And some of themselves admitted the conviction that they were far sunk from the power and purity of the Apostles of Christ, and were preaching about a salvation which they had not in possession.

Another important train of ideas arose from searching the scriptures. There was a falling away spoken of by Christ and his Apostles, and an antichrist to rise, which appeared according to history, to have taken place a great while ago. And it appeared by many promises, that after the reign of this antichrist was out, there would be glorious times upon earth, and Christ would appear again and set up his kingdom, and gather the nations into it. Here many enquiries were raised, concerning the reign of this antichrist: when it began and when it would end, and when Christ would appear and set up his true kingdom. And many began to apprehend, that this period was not far off; and concluded it was time to leave off their vain disputes, and unite in prayer for Christ to come and pour out his [13] spirit, gather his people into one, make an end of sin, and fill the earth with his glory.

VII. For several years there were praying societies kept up in different parts, composed of persons who were distinguished in some things from all the denominations; though blended with them in their outward communion. These professed to be in search of the truth and power of religion, and ready to embrace it whenever it should appear; but did not believe it to be among any of the denominations, in purity. They believed there were errors in all their systems of doctrine, which kept them dead and lifeless, without the spirit of God. The social exercises which sprung from this faith, were reading the scriptures without any comment, praying for the divine spirit to open them, confessing and lamenting the deplorable state of mankind in general, and that of cold, lifeless and corrupt professors of Christianity in particular; and pleading for the accomplishment of those blessed promises which respected the coming of Christ and the glory of the latter days. Examining themselves by the evidences and marks of grace laid down in the scriptures, lamenting a lack of those evidences, confessing their short comings in duty, and resolving to correct past errors, and be more watchful over a deceitful and desperately wicked heart, opening their trials to one another, and encouraging each other to persevere until they found Christ in every deed.

When any one prays for a thing, it is sure and certain evidence that he has not that thing in possession: and hence the united prayers of hundreds of the warmest professors, entreating Christ to come and visit the churches, loudly proclaimed that he was not already there. While he was contemplated at a distance through the promise, the following lines well suited the day, and proved his absence from the soul:

"When I turn my eyes within;
All is dark, and vain, and wild:
Full of unbelief and sin;
Can I deem myself a child?" [14]

The following extracts of letters from persons of no small note in the churches, will show more particularly the state of religion at that period.

March 22, 1798
"MY DEAR FRIEND, I HAVE this winter past, preached with difficulty, my heart but little engaged. I know that I am not as I ought to be, yet cannot be effected with my sad case." W. R.

"DEAR SIR, YESTERDAY I received your kind letter, and I now undertake to answer it."
"The dead state of religion is truly discouraging here, as well as elsewhere. It appears a wonder of mercy, that God is so kind to this *Sardis,* as to afford her the means of grace; without this she would certainly run into total infidelity. When I look into my wretched heart and consider how much I have dishonored God, by dead and careless life, I have reason to cover my head in the dust."
"If some are spotted with sin, I am spotted all over." J. T.

Lexington, Sept. 5, 1796.
"DEAR BROTHER, It is not likely I can say anything to entertain or refresh you. I sometimes think I would be willing to travel with you to heaven, but I feel very unlike an inhabitant of that place. I would be glad to be at the *truth* and the *substance."*

"But I commonly feel so much more like a Devil than a Christian, that it makes me often forebode the displeasure of God, the holy, and the just. I sometimes think I am coming towards the birth, but can seldom think I am born. O how long! how long! And what am I? I would strip off everything but [15] Christ and his holy spirit, to enter the narrow gate."

"I can tell you but little about my poor congregations. I see but little prospect of encouragement. I dare not say none. I sometimes hope to see Jesus King in Zion. J. D. "

VIII. Now let any one judge from the foregoing evidences, what kind of work was necessary to take place among *such a people,* in order to their recovery; a people confessedly, *vain, and dark, and wild; full of unbelief and sin, dead and careless, spot all over;* and *more like devils than Christians.*

The generality, however, unaffected with their *sad case,* were still going on, crying out against infidelity, lampooning the Deist, treating his cavils with contempt and laboring each one to augment his party: while a distressed few were watching, like the guards of the night and ready to meet the first dawn of the approaching day.

A sense of total depravity of human nature, and the entire separation of the soul from God, is the first thing necessary to prepare the way for the entrance of spiritual life. Therefore, such as honestly confessed their lost and deplorable state, and intensely groaned for deliverance from it, were not in so dangerous a condition as those who made a high-sounding *profession,* and gloried in some *plan* of salvation that still left them in bondage to corruption. But a conviction of being lost, never saved any one, though many have made conviction a great evidence of their election, and vainly rested upon that light which searches out the evil and wickedness of the heart, without going any further. But such as were honest before God, could not stop here, they must be at the *truth* and the *substance*. Therefore, it was necessary that the channel through which the quickening power of God has access to the [16] soul, should be opened: namely, *the everlasting covenant of redemption*. And as this is the only channel through which souls can receive any special favor from God, it will be proper here to make a few observations concerning it.

IX. When one makes a promise to another, and that promise is accepted; this constitutes a *covenant* or *agreement*. Thus the promise of eternal life was made to Christ, before the foundation of the world, and accepted by him in behalf of all his seed. In this promise, or *covenant of life,* the *Father* and *Son* were perfectly united; and as both are everlasting and unchangeable, it must be an everlasting and unchangeable *covenant* which cannot be broken. The *covenant* itself, is absolute, unconditional and inviolable. But in order to its being fulfilled and finally settled, there is a work given to the *Son* to do, which in the nature of things, is necessary to be done; and that is, to overcome *death,* and *him* that has the power of it. And until this is actually done, the heir is in bondage. It is true, *eternal life* is secured in the *covenant,* to all the seed; though they be not in actual possession of it. But while death reigns, the blessings of the *covenant* can only be administered by way of *promise;* and the party to whom the *promise* shall be fulfilled, designated in the *Father's revealed will.*

This *everlasting covenant* has ever been a mystery to man in his fallen state, nor could anything certain be ever known respecting it but by a *living revelation* from God, an express manifestation of the divine will, attested by *living witnesses.* And where this orderly administration has been wanting, the more that has been said about it, the greater the confusion and controversy has been stirred up.

It is true, the scriptures contain a *copy* of the *divine will,* concerning the redemption of souls: all the promises of God are there recorded. But of what use is a bare *copy* of a will, without *witnesses?* [17]

These great and precious *promises* could effect nothing real; the inheritance itself was not in them; and although thousands have undertaken to administer upon the authority of the scripture, as though it was the very *original itself,* sealed and confirmed by unalterable seals, and have pretended to be the *true witnesses* of God; yet their folly is made manifest to all men, for they have not agreed in their witness but have filled the world with endless debates, concerning the sense and meaning of what *they* call the *will.* Now if the witnesses were all divided, and could not even agree in their testimony who were the proper heirs, how could anything ever be decided in such a court?

But however great the contention has been about the *copy;* and however much these presumers have altered, amended, expounded and paraphrased upon it, yet the *original* has remained unsullied. God is of one mind, and his promises in Christ, are Yea and Amen.

When God revealed his covenant to Abraham, it was only by promise. "*In thee and in thy seed, shall all the nations of the earth be blessed.*" OBSERVE; the blessing promised, was not to *Abraham and his seed;* but to *all the nations of the earth.* It was not, *Thou and thy seed* shall be blessed with irresistible grace, but "*In thee and in thy seed* [which is Christ] *all the nations of the earth shall be blessed.*" All were under the curse, and stood in equal need of the blessing. *Sin* and *death* had their dominions equally over all. But a better dominion was promised; a kingdom of righteousness; a dominion of life; in which *all the nations of the earth should be blessed.*

Although death reigned from Adam to Moses, and from Moses to Christ; yet the promise of God to Abraham, was sure to all the seed; *death* could not destroy it; the *law* could not supplant it, or make it void; the threatenings and curses from mount Sinai, were not against the *promise* nor the *seed,* to whom the promise was made. The promise was established and confirmed by [18] unalterable seals, illustrated by types and figures, and attested by a long succession of living Prophets, until Christ the proper heir made his appearance; finished the work that was given him to do, received the substance that was promised by the Father, and took possession of the *inheritance.* Until this took place, souls were in bondage under the rudiments of the world; they could find no resurrection into eternal life, until the son of God, in the fullness of time, was made of a woman; made flesh; placed under the same rudiments by which they were held in bondage; and from thence ascended step by step, until he entered the promised possession. Then, and not until then, the way was open for the substance to be ministered; then the first born could give gifts unto his brethren, substantial, real gifts. What he received of the Father, he gave to those who were joint heirs with him to the *promised possession,* and sent them into the world as he had been sent, to minister to others as he ministered to them. Moreover, he did not send them to some particular persons, but to every creature that was under heaven; and commissioned them *to proclaim liberty to the captives, and the opening of the prison to them that are bound;* one as much as another. No nation or individual was excluded, but the promise was to all, and upon all, and should finally be fulfilled to all them that *believe and obey.*

X. While the everlasting covenant was thus ministered in truth by the Apostles and true witnesses of Christ, it was confirmed by the most convincing signs, wonders, miracles, and gifts of the Holy Ghost. They healed the sick, raised the dead, cast out malignant spirits, spoke with unknown tongues, held converse with angels and departed spirits, saw visions, fell into trances, had gifts of prophesying, etc. etc. These, and such like, were *seals* to their ministry. But above all, the salutary charge produced in the lives and manners of those who believed, confirmed the doctrine to be of God; and served as a *test* to those who should come after, whereby to distinguish the *true covenant* of God, from all the *counterfeit doctrines* of men. When the true [19] administration of the covenant ceased, the signs and seals of confirmation ceased with it. God would not affix his seal to the canons, decrees and covenants of wicked men, who rose up to supplant the true work of redemption. And therefore for many ages, what has been called the *Christian doctrine,* has been void of authority, except what arises from superstition, vain philosophy, the power of human eloquence, or the civil sword. But when God, in infinite kindness, began to revive the everlasting truth in these latter days, the living seals of the covenant were annexed. Such seals and evidences of a supernatural and divine power, as have excited as great astonishment in the minds of mankind, as those of antiquity.

Chapter Two

Of the first appearance of the extraordinary work, in different parts of Kentucky, in 1800 *and* 1801.
Original pages 19-28

THE first extraordinary appearances of the power of God in the late revival, began about the close of the last century, in Logan and Christian counties; on the waters of Gasper and Red Rivers. And in the spring of 1801, the same extraordinary work broke out in Mason county, upper part of Kentucky; of which I was an eye witness, and can therefore, with greater confidence, testify what I have heard, seen and felt.

It first began in individuals who had been under deep convictions of sin, and great trouble about their souls, and had fasted and prayed, and diligently searched the scriptures, and had undergone distresses of mind inexpressibly sore, until they had obtained a comfortable hope of salvation. And from seeing and feeling the love of Christ, and his willingness to save all that would forsake their sins and turn to God through him; and feeling how freely his love and goodness flowed [20] to them, it kindled their love to other souls, that were lost in their sins; and an ardent desire that they might come and partake of that spiritual light, life, and comfort, which appeared infinite in its nature, and free to all. And under such and overpowering weight of the divine goodness, as tongue could not express, they were constrained to cry out, with tears and trembling, and testify a full and free salvation in Christ, for all that would come; and to warn their fellow creatures of the danger of continuing in sin; and entreating them in the most tender and affectionate manner, to turn from it; and seek the Lord, in sure and certain hope that he would be found.

Under such exhortations, the people began to be affected in a very strange manner. At first they were taken with an inward throbbing of the heart; then with weeping and trembling: from that to crying out, in apparent agony of the soul; falling down and swooning away till every appearance of animal life was suspended, and the person appeared to be in a trance. From this state they would recover under different sensations, which will be more particularly noticed hereafter.

The following extract of a letter, dated Caneridge, Jan. 30, 1801, give a striking account of the work; as it first appeared in the lower parts of Kentucky and Cumberland:

"The work is still increasing in Cumberland: It has overspread the whole country. It is in Nashville, Barren, Muddy, Gasper, Redbanks, Knoxville, etc."

"J. M. C. has been there two months; he says it exceeds any he ever saw or heard of. Children and all, seem to be engaged: but children are the most active in the work. When they speak, it appears that the Lord sends his spirit to accompany it with power to the hearts of sinners. They all seem to be wrought in an extraordinary way; lie as though they were dead, for some time; without pulse or breath; some longer, some a shorter time. Some rise with joy and triumph; others crying for mercy. As soon as they get comfort, they cry to [21] sinners, exhorting them day and night to turn to the Lord." P. H.

It is worthy of notice, that a work by which God intended to bring down the pride and loftiness of man, should begin in small children. By this it was manifest who were

Chapter 2

the furthest lost from God, and what course must be taken, in order to return.

At a sacrament, near Flemingsburgh, the last Sabbath in April, the power of God was very visible among the people through the whole of the occasion; under which there was much weeping, trembling and convulsion of soul: But what was the most solemn and striking, was the case of two little girls, who in the time of meeting, cried out in great distress. They both continued for some time praying and crying for mercy, till one of them received a comfortable hope; and then turning to the other, cried out "O! you little sinner, come to Christ! take hold of his promise! trust in him! he is able to save to the uttermost! O! I have found peace in my soul! O! the precious Savior! Come just as you are! He will take away the stony heart and give you a heart of flesh! You can't make yourself any better, Just give up your heart to Christ, now! You are not a greater sinner than me! You need not wait another moment!" Thus she continued exhorting, until her little companion received a ray from heaven, that produced a sudden and sensible change: then rising with her in her arms, she cried out in a most affecting manner, "O here is another star of light!" These children were perhaps nine or ten years old. The Sabbath following about twenty persons were struck in the congregation of Cabin-Creek, Mason county. Among the first who cried out in distress, was a girl about twelve years old. Their convictions of their lost state, (from a sudden opening of that pure holiness to which sin stands directly opposed) were quick as a lightning's flash; and came with such weight, that had they not, in some way or other, opened their case, they must have sunk into [22] the horrors of despair. It was dire necessity which at first obliged them to expose themselves to public view as objects of pity, for everything of the kind, was looked upon by the generality, even of professors, as wild enthusiasm, or the fruits of a disordered brain.

There were however a few who understood the disorder, and were ready to fly to their relief and proclaim liberty to the captives, and the opening of the prison to them that were bound.

And here a new scene was opened, while some trembled like one in a fit of the fever, wept and cried out, lamenting their distance from God, and exposedness to his wrath; others were employed in praying with them, encouraging them to believe on the Son of God, to venture upon his promise, give up their wicked rebellious heart, just as it was; for God to take it away, and give them a heart of flesh; singing hymns, and giving thanks to God, for the display of his power, without any regard to former rules of order. At this, some were offended and withdrew from the assembly, determined to oppose it, as a work of the wicked one. But all their objections only tended to open the way for the true nature and spirit of the work to shine out; and encourage the subjects of it, to set out with warmer zeal to promote it. Accordingly a meeting was appointed a few evenings after, to which a crowd of awakened souls flocked, and spent the whole night in singing hymns, praying, and exhorting one another, etc. At this meeting, one man was struck down and lay for about an hour, in the situation above mentioned. This put the matter beyond dispute, that the work was supernatural; and the outcry which it raised against sin, confirmed a number in the belief that it was from above.

From these small beginnings, it gradually spread. The news of these strange operations flew abroad, and attracted many to come and see; who were convinced, not only from seeing and hearing, but feeling; and carried home the testimony, that it was the living work of God. This stirred up others, and brought out still greater multitudes. And these strange exercises still increasing, [23] and having no respect to any stated hours of worship, it was found expedient to encamp on the ground and continue the meeting day and

Chapter 2

night. To these encampments the people flocked in hundreds and thousands, on foot, on horseback, and in wagons and other carriages.

At first appearance, those meetings exhibited nothing to the spectator, but a scene of confusion that could scarce be put into human language. They were generally opened with a sermon; near the close of which, there would be an unusual out-cry; some bursting forth into loud ejaculations of prayer, or thanksgiving for the truth: Others breaking out in emphatic sentences of exhortation: Others flying to their careless friends, with tears of compassion, beseeching them to turn to the Lord. Some struck with terror, and hastening through the crowd to make their escape, or pulling away their relations. Others, trembling, weeping and crying out for the Lord Jesus to have mercy upon them: fainting and swooning away, till every appearance of life was gone, and the extremities of the body assumed the coldness of a dead corpse. Others surrounding them with melodious songs, or fervent prayers for their happy resurrection in the love of Christ. Others collecting into circles around this variegated scene, contending with arguments for and against. And under such appearances, the work would continue for several days and nights together.

I shall now mention particularly, some of the first meetings of this kind, with a few accompanying circumstances, from which the work took a general spread in the year 1801.

The first was held at Cabin-Creek. It began on the 22nd of May, and continued four days and three nights. The scene was awful beyond description; the falling, crying out, praying, exhorting, singing, shouting, etc. exhibited such new and striking evidences of a supernatural power, that few, if any could escape without being affected. Such as tried to run from it, were frequently struck on the way, or impelled by some alarming signal to return: and so powerful was the evidence [24] on all sides, that no place was found for the obstinate sinner to shelter himself, but under the protection of prejudiced and bigoted professors. No circumstance at this meeting, appeared more striking, than the great numbers that fell on the third night: and to prevent their being trodden under foot by the multitude, they were collected together and laid out in order, on two squares of the meeting-house; which, like so many dead corpses, covered a considerable part of the floor. There were persons at this meeting, from Caneridge, Concord, Eagle-Creek, and other neighboring congregations, who partook of the spirit of the work, which was a particular means of its spreading.

The next general camp-meeting was held at Concord, in the county of Bourbon, about the last of May, or beginning of June. The number of people was supposed to be about 4,000, who attended on this occasion. There were present seven Presbyterian ministers; four of whom were opposed to the work, and spoke against it until the fourth day about noon; the evidence then became so powerful, that they all professed to be convinced, that it was the work of God; and one of them addressed the assembly with tears, acknowledging, that notwithstanding they had long been praying to the Lord to pour out his spirit, yet when it came, they did not know it, but wickedly opposed the answer of their own prayers. On this occasion, no sex nor color, class nor description, were exempted from the pervading influence of the spirit; even from the age of eight months, to sixty years, there were evident subjects of this marvelous operation.

The meeting continued five days, and four nights; and after the people generally scattered from the ground, numbers convened in different places, and continued the exercise much longer. And even where they were not collected together, these wonderful operations continued among every class of people, and in every situation; in their houses and fields, and in their daily employments: falling down and crying out under conviction, or singing and shouting with unspeakable joy, were so common, that the whole country round about, seemed to be leavened with the spirit of the work. [25]

The next camp meeting was at Eagle-Creek, Adams county, Ohio. It began June 5, and continued four days and three nights. The number of people there was not so great, as the country was new, but the work was equally powerful according to the number. At this meeting the principal leading characters in that place fully embraced the spirit of the work, which laid a permanent foundation for its continuance and spread in that quarter.

The next general meeting was at Pleasant Point, Kentucky which equaled if not surpassed any that had been before. Here, the Christian minister, so called; the common professor; the professed deist and degenerate, were forced to take one common lot among the wounded, and confess with equal candor, that hitherto they had been total strangers to the religion of Jesus. From this meeting, the work was spread extensively through Bourbon, Fayette, and other neighboring counties, and was carried by a number of its subjects to the south side of Kentucky, where it found a permanent residence in the hearts of many.

The general meeting at Indian creek, Harrison county, began the 24th of July, and continued about five days and nights. To this meeting, the subjects of the work were generally collected from all quarters, and abundantly strengthened each other in the indiscriminate exercises of prayer, exhortation, singing, shouting and leaping for joy. But there was very little appearance of that power which strikes conviction to the heart of the sinner, until the third day about two o'clock in the afternoon. A boy from appearance about twelve years old, retired from the stand in time of preaching under a very extraordinary impression, and having mounted a log at some distance, and raising his voice in a very affecting manner, he attracted the main body of the people in a few minutes. With tears streaming from his eyes, he cried aloud to the wicked, warning them of their danger, denouncing their certain doom if they persisted in their sins, expressing his love to their souls, and desire that they would turn to the Lord and be saved. [26] He was held up by two men, and spoke for about an hour, with that convincing eloquence that could be inspired only from above. When his strength seemed quite exhausted and language failed to describe the feelings of his soul, he raised his hand and dropping his handkerchief, wet from sweat from his little face, cried out, "Thus, O sinner! Shall you drop into hell, unless you forsake your sins and turn to the Lord." At that moment some fell like those who are shot in battle, and the work spread in a manner which human language cannot describe.

The next general meeting was at Caneridge, Bourbon county, seven miles from Paris. It began the 6th of August, and continued day and night about a week. The number of people collected on the ground at once, was supposed to be about twenty thousand; but it was thought a much greater number were there in the course of the meeting. The encampment consisted of one hundred and thirty-five wheel-carriages and tents proportioned to the people. This immense group included almost every character that could be named, but amidst them all, the subjects of this new and strange operation, were distinguished by their flaming zeal for the destruction of sin, and the deliverance of souls from its power. The various operations and exercises on that occasion, were indescribable. The falling exercises was the most noted. James Crawford, one of the oldest ministers in the state, and one of the foremost in the work, informed me that he kept as accurate an account as he could of the number that fell on the occasion, and computed it to be about three thousand. The vast numbers who received light on this occasion, and went forth in every direction to spread it, render it impossible to pursue any further the particular track of progress. I shall only add that it was but a few weeks after this meeting, that the same work broke out in North Carolina, by the instrumentality of some who went from Caneridge to bear the testimony.[1] [27]

I shall now take notice of the opposition which was raised against the work in this first stage of it, and show some of the causes from which it sprung.

The people among whom the revival began, were generally Calvinists, and although they had been long praying in words for the out-pouring of the spirit, and believed that God had *"foreordained whatsoever comes to pass;"* yet, when it *came to pass* that their prayer was answered and the spirit began to flow like many waters, from a cloud of witnesses, and souls were convicted of sin and cried for mercy, and found hope and comfort in the news of a Savior; they rose up and quarreled with the work, because it did not *come to pass* that the subjects of it were willing to adopt their souls stupefying creed. Those who have labored and travailed to gain some solid hope of salvation, and had ventured their souls upon the covenant of promise, and felt the living seal of eternal love; could not, dare not preach that salvation was restricted to a certain *definite number;* nor insinuate that any being which God had made, was, by the Creator, laid under the dire necessity of being damned forever. The love of a Savior constrained them to testify, that one had died for all. This truth, so essential to the first ray of hope in the human breast, was like a dead fly in the ointment of the apothecary, to the Calvinist; hence all this trembling, weeping and groaning under sin, rejoicing in the hope of deliverance and turning from the former practice of it, sent forth a disagreeable savor. Yet these exercises would no doubt, have passed for a good work of God, had they appeared as seals to their doctrine of election, imperfection, and final perseverance. But everything appeared new, and to claim no relation to the old bed of sand upon which they had been building; and rather than quit the old foundation, they chose to reject, oppose and persecute the truth, accompanied with all [28] that evidence which many of them were obliged to acknowledge was divine.

Some who were inwardly opposed, at first exercised forbearance, and professed a measure of union with the work, in hopes that it would die away like former revivals, and the people return to their old order. But as they perceived that it increased, they laid aside the mask, and came out with a bold testimony against it, as a dangerous delusion.

In some of the churches there were days set apart for fasting and prayer, to deprecate the divine displeasure, through which they supposed it was sent upon the land.

These public testimonies against the work, particularly by ministers, were a means of stirring up and encouraging those who were openly wicked, to come forth and mock, oppose, and persecute; but even such, were often unable to withstand the power, and sometimes in the very act of persecuting and afflicting, were struck down like men in battle; and so alarming was the sight, that others on foot or on horseback, would try to make their escape and flee away like those who are closely pursued by an enemy in time of war, and be overtaken by the invisible power, under which they would be struck down and constrained to cry out in anguish, and confess their wickedness in persecuting the work of God, and warn others not to oppose it. Thus, many who were openly profane, were taken in the very act of persecuting the work, and like Saul of Tarsus, made the happy subjects and zealous promoters of it; while bigoted professors, who had hissed them on, remained *like the heath in the desert, that seeth not when good cometh.*

{1} One person in particular here alluded to, who went on this important mission, was JOHN RANKIN, Minister of the Presbyterian church at Gasper, Logan county; the first who received the spirit of the revival in that place, and under whose ministry the extraordinary work began.

Chapter 2

Since that time he has escaped from the old house of the antichrist, divided against itself and with the major part of his Gasper congregation, embraced the Gospel of Christ's second appearing.

Chapter Three

Of the distinguishing doctrines and manner of worship, among the first subjects of the revival.
Original Pages 29-40

THE first point of doctrine which distinguished the subjects of the revival, was that which respected divine revelation.

The established opinion in the churches had been, that the *Scriptures,* explained according to sound reason and philosophy, was light sufficient; and simply to believe, what we were thus taught, was the highest evidence we could have of the truth of spiritual things. But *these* adopted a very different faith, and taught, as an important truth, that the will of God was made manifest to each individual who honestly sought after it, by an inward light, which shone into the heart. Hence they received the name of *New Lights.* Those who were the subjects of this inward light, did not call it *new light,* but a renewed manifestation of *that,* which at sundry times and in divers manners, had been opened to those who were willing and desirous to know the truth for themselves.

This inward light, they denominated [referred to as] *the Lord,* because by it they were instructed, influenced and governed. Hence they spoke of seeking *the Lord,* finding *the Lord,* loving *the Lord,* following *the Lord,* offending *the Lord,* etc. by all which expressions was meant, that *inward light* and revelation of the truth, by which they could see things in their true colors, and find a measure of peace and consolation, and a comfortable hope of eternal life.

II. This *new light* first broke out in the Presbyterian church, among those who held doctrines of Calvin, and therefore it is considered as more immediately contrasted with that system. Those who first embraced it, had also been reputed Calvinists, and [30] belonged to the Presbyterian church, among whom were several persons of distinction in the ministry; of course, the existence of sentiments so very different in the same church, rendered a division unavoidable. This division was gradual, and had its foundation in the above principle of a direct manifestation of spiritual light from God to the soul, which was superior to all the comments that natural men had ever made upon the scriptures. This division in sentiment, with its accompanying effects, drew together a vast multitude out of different churches, who formed a general communion, and for a time, acceded to the doctrines, manner of worship, etc. first opened and practiced among the *New Lights;* a brief sketch of which is as follows, viz.: That all creeds, confessions, forms of worship, and rules of government invented by men, ought to be laid aside; especially the distinguishing doctrines of Calvin. That all who received the true light of the spirit in the inner man, and faithfully followed it, would naturally see eye to eye, and understand the things of the spirit alike, without any written tenet or learned expositor. That all who received this true light, would plainly see the purity of God, the depravity of man, the necessity of a new birth, and of a sinless life and conversation to evidence it, That God was no respecter of persons, desires the salvation of all souls, has opened a door of salvation through Christ, for all, will have all invited to enter, and such as refuse to come in, must blame themselves for their own perdition.

III. As to worship, they allowed each one to worship God, agreeably to their own feelings, whatever impression or consciousness of duty they were under: believing the true wisdom, which "lives through all life," to be a safer guide than human forms, which can only affect the outer man: and hence, so wide a door was opened, and such a variety of exercises were exhibited in their public meetings. All distinction of names was laid aside, and it was no matter what any one had been called before, if now he stood in the present light, and felt his heart glow with love to the souls of men; [31] he was welcome to sing, pray, or call sinners to repentance. Neither was there any distinction as to age, sex, color, or anything of a temporary nature: old and young, male and female, black and white, had equal privilege to minister the light which they received, in whatever way the spirit directed. And moreover generally considered, that such as professed to stand in the light and were not actively engaged some way or other, in time of public meeting, were only dead weights upon the cause.

IV. No one, who has not been an eye witness, can possibly paint in their imagination the striking solemnity of those occasions, on which the thousands of Kentuckians were convened in one vast assembly, under the auspicious influence of the above faith. How striking to see hundreds who never saw each other in the face before, moving uniformly into action, without any preconceived plan, and each, without intruding upon another, taking that part assigned him by a conscious feeling, and in this manner, dividing into bands over a large extent of ground, interspersed with tents and wagons. Some uniting their voices in the most melodious songs; others in solemn and affecting accents of prayer: some lamenting with streaming eyes their lost situation, or that of the wicked world; others lying apparently in the cold embraces of death: some instructing the ignorant, directing the doubtful, and urging them in the day of God's visitation, to make sure work for eternity: others, from some eminence, sounding the general trump of a free salvation, and warning sinners to fly from the wrath to come: the surrounding forest at the same time, vocal with the cries of the distressed, sometimes to the distance of half a mile or a mile in circumference.

How persons, so different in their education, manners and natural dispositions, without any visible commander, could enter upon such a scene, and continue in it for days and nights in perfect harmony, has been one of the greatest wonders that ever the world beheld; and was no doubt included in the visions of [32] that man, who, falling into a trance with his eyes open, cried out, "*How goodly are thy tents, O Jacob! and thy tabernacles, O Israel! as the valleys are they spread forth, as gardens by the river's side; as the trees of lign-aloes, which the Lord hath planted.*" [Num 24:5-6]

V. The supernatural and extraordinary gifts of the spirit which were visible among this people, are not less worthy of notice than their distinguishing faith and manner of worship; such as left no remaining doubt of the restitution of that sacred armor, which, together with the apostolic faith, had been trodden under foot for many hundred years by the power of antichrist. To evince this, as the faith of that people at least, I insert a few extracts of their writings.

David Purviance, in a letter dated Caneridge, March 1, 1802, writes thus:

"Some things have lately taken place among us, which I think more extraordinary than any I have seen or heard since the apostolic age. The case of Rachel Martin, was truly miraculous. I suppose you have heard of it."

This extraordinary case is illustrated by the following extract from another hand:

"Last Saturday exceeded by far anything I ever saw before. Rachel Martin was struck the Thursday night after you left this: She never eat nor spoke for nine days and nights. I was there when she rose and spoke: her countenance was as it were, refined (i.e. transfigured). She told me she was free from the world all that time: She says the work will increase." P. H.

Aeneas M'Callister, in a letter dated, May, 1802, speaking of the work in North-Carolina, observes,

"The like wonders have not been seen, except the KENTUCKY REVIVAL last summer, since the Apostle's days. I suppose the exercises of our congregation this last winter, surpassed anything ever seen or heard of. I sometimes think it would have been well, if they had been kept in and never told."

It is certain, the natural man receives not the things of the spirit of God, for they are foolishness to him; hence Christ instructed his disciples not [33] to cast pearls before swine; for the same cause, so little has been published abroad concerning the deep things of God, made manifest among the people called *New Lights:* and for the same reason, these things can be but slightly touched at present.

VI. That the power was supernatural by which such multitudes were struck down, required no arguments to prove; and had they never risen again, their might have been some reason for charging it to the devil: but who has the power to kill and make alive again? could any one with the rationality of a man, suppose that anything short of the power of God, could suspend the functions of animal life for an hour, a day, or a week, and again restore them with additional brightness?, Is nature wont to assume such apparent changes, as for tens and fifties, moved at the same time by the same instinct, to forget the use of every limb, and prostrate fall no matter where, and yawn, and grasp, and expire in a cold sweat? This belongs not to nature, and as little does it belong to nature to exempt her sons from wounds and bruises, broken limbs, and aching heads, in case of such repeated and dangerous falls as were common among the *New Lights*. And least of all, could nature's power extend to their resurrection, after an hour, a week, or nine days in a trance. Who wants a miracle to arouse their faith, and fix it on the sacred truths recorded in the scriptures; let him recognize the camp-meeting, let him find the man, or woman, whose immortal part for hours and days traversed the regions of eternity, while the breathless body lay as a spectacle of terror to surrounding friends.

The learned expositor of scripture and the one whom he scornfully terms an infidel, are equally baffled with the falling exercise; the one upon his hypothesis, that there never was such a thing as a miracle in the days of the apostles; and the other, that there never was to be any such thing after. All their experiments and researches were in vain, to reduce this operation to some natural cause. Their feeling the pulse, changing the situation of the person, applying the smelling bottles, bathing with henna, or cold water, letting of blood, etc. could never [34] make half the discovery in the case that those made who came with their barrels of whisky to retail out to the multitude.

By such it was abundantly proved, that the readiest way to keep clear of this extraordinary exercise, was to drown the soul in debauchery and vice. Many circumstances, beating and confounding to the wisdom of man, attended the exercises mentioned, which for sake of brevity have to be omitted. And yet however extraordinary these things were, they were not considered by the people as the most evidential of a work of the true spirit: something much greater was commonly expected to succeed their resurrection, of greater importance than anything that went before. The word of exhortation is ranked among the apostolic gifts, and as such it was considered by the *New Lights*.

This gift was generally expected on the occasion of rising from the before mentioned trance, and such expectations were very commonly answered. The exhortations delivered on those occasions by all ranks and colors, but especially by small children, were so evidential of a divine power, so searching to the conscience, so wounding to the sinner, that the most obstinate unbelievers have fallen down, like those of old, and confessed that God was in them of a truth.

It required a spirit more incredulous, than that which has commonly been called infidelity, to deny a supernatural agency in the case of such compassionate and powerful addresses from little children, not only unlearned, but also of the most bashful and unpopular cast of mind. Such little ones, of eight or ten years old, raised upon the shoulders or held up in the arms of some one, in the midst of vast multitudes, would speak in a manner so marvelous and astonishing, that persons of the most rugged passions would dissolve into tears; and professors of the foremost rank, confess that hitherto they had been total strangers to that heavenly sense and feeling, which so distinguished a child of God. So deep were the effects of truth, delivered in the simple language of a child, of which the following may serve as a short specimen.

"O the sweetness of redeeming love! O if sinners [35] "knew the sweetness of redeeming love, they would all come to the overflowing fountain!"

The general gift of exhortation was to search out the state of the sinner, convict him of sin, and warn him to fly from it; and they often came so pointed, even to naming out the person and publicly arraigning him for specific crimes, that often evil spirits, whose work it is to cover iniquity, and conceal it, were stirred up to great fury; and those possessed with them, would come forth in a great rage, threatening and blaspheming against the author of the revival, and bold as Goliath, challenge his armies to an encounter. Could nature, without bloodshed and slaughter, overcome beings so fierce? Or must it not be something supernatural? To see a bold Kentuckian (undaunted by the horrors of war) turn pale and tremble at the reproof of a weak woman, a little boy, or a mean African; to see him sink down in deep remorse, roll and toss, and gnash his teeth, till black in the face; entreat the prayers of those he came to devour, and through their fervent intercessions and kind instructions, obtain deliverance, and return in the possession of the meek and gentle spirit which he set out to oppose: who would say the change was not supernatural and miraculous? Such exorcisms, or casting out of evil spirits, are justly ranked among the wonders which attended the *New-Light:* Nor could the man once delivered from the *Legion,* go home with greater joy to tell his friends what great things Jesus has done for him, than many returned from these encamping grounds, to announce to their former companions, their happy change.

VII. To what has been said it may be objected, that many who were converted in this extraordinary manner, gave no lasting evidence of a real change, but returned again to their former courses; and as they testified that they were all actuated by one spirit, if some were mistaken, why not the whole?

I answer, the work of God is one thing and the opinion formed by the subject of it, another. If it should be granted that many, or even all, were mistaken as [36] to the immediate effect of the work, this would not alter the work from what it was. If a foolish person should take grain when it was only in the blossom, and say it was ripe, and go to reaping, binding and stacking it, this would not prove that the plowing and sowing had not been well done by a good farmer. Spiritual life is of a growing nature, as well as vegetable and animal life; and if many, zealous to increase the number of their disciples, did deceive the generality with a vain persuasion, that a short scene of conviction, light and comfort, comprehended all that was contained in the new birth, and cut them off from any further growth, this did not prove that their impressions had not a proper beginning, or were not of the genuine kind.

Obj. 2. If this great appearance of union and general communion was of God, why did it not increase? *Ans.* Why did not that union and communion increase which existed among the Pharisees, Sadducees, Essenes, Herodians and Syrophoenicians, who followed Christ into the wilderness and encamped there day and night? The reason is plain, the foundation of a lasting union could not be laid until the rubbish was cleared out of the way, and as this was the first work then, so it was in the late revival; those who followed the true light were united in breaking down and burning that which was old and rotten, and this had to be done before they could unite in building up that which is sound and permanent. So that a union in the first case, although it is productive of greater division, yet is both a shadow and a sure pledge of that union which follows in consequence.

Obj. 3. But what do you make of those who testified that they had got all the rubbish destroyed, were carried above all sin, and temptation, and pain, and never should suffer again, were higher than Elijah, perfectly blessed and filled with the fullness of God; and with all this so united in heart that they never could part, etc. and yet after all, turn to hate one another worse than ever, and live as loose and wicked as others? So that they could afterwards say: [37]

> "*Ah! Where am I now! When was it, or how,*
> *That I fell from my heaven of grace?*
> *I am striped of my all, I am brought into thrall,*
> *I am banished from Jesus' face."*

Do not such changes prove that their extraordinary light was all a delusion? Ans. If so, the same argument will prove that every dispensation of light, both under that law and Gospel was a delusion, for after the brightest manifestations there was always a falling away. Did not the whole camp of Israel fall away after the giving of the law upon mount Sinai? But did this prove that the light they saw there, and all the signs and wonders that preceded and accompanied it, was delusion? David, Solomon, and all the Kings and people of Israel fell away; and how often was this chosen generation brought under judgments and banished into captivity, not to prove that their extraordinary light had been all delusion, but the contrary.

John the Baptist decreased and his followers came to nothing; and all that had followed Jesus for three years, forsook him and fell away in the hour of trial. If this was not sufficient according to the above objection to prove their light a delusion, you may add the universal apostasy that prevailed through the long reign of antichrist, in which *there was none that did good and sinned not, no not one.* Now if the same visible consequences have attended this kind of light first and last, the different manifestations of it must be established or condemned together. But to obviate [sic] the question more particularly, it will be proper to observe, that divine light is first received by faith.

We must first believe the report concerning things invisible, before we can see the object face to face and actually possess it; and the firm belief of a thing will produce great effects both on the mind and body. *Whom having not seen, ye love, in whom believing, though now ye see him not, yet rejoice with joy unspeakable and full of glory.* This unspeakable joy was merely the fruit of faith in those who had yet to *receive the end of their faith, even the salvation of the soul.* Now if those called *New Lights* did testify that they were dead to the world, [38] and risen with Christ above all sin, temptation, pain and suffering, were full of glory and perfectly blessed with the fullness of God, united in heart, and beyond the possibility of a separation, they only meant that this was their situation by faith; i. e. they had full faith that such a state was attainable, and were swallowed up in the delightful contemplation of it, as though they were actually in it. But that it was not their real situation, was evident from their repeated complaints of remaining darkness, and their prayers for returning light.

If it is said that upon this principle, all their exercises were only the workings of imagination: I answer, that until a thing is brought present to the senses, the brightest knowledge we can have of it is a bright and clear imagination, by means of a shadow or image of the thing. But we must distinguish between a vain imagination and that which is properly founded. If we form an imagination of a thing that has no existence, that imagination is vain; but it is not so, when the image of a thing is drawn upon the mind which has actual existence. What knowledge had the Jews of the kingdom of Christ while under the ceremonial law, beyond the effect of lively images? *The law having a shadow of good things to come, and not the very substance of the things, could never with those sacrifices which they offered year by year continually, make the comers thereunto perfect, for would they not then have ceased to be offered?* Observe their imagination were not in vain, they were *shadows of good things, of real substances,* although they were yet to come, and absolutely necessary to come in order to their perfection.

Now the cases are perfectly similar, for if the *New Lights* had found *real perfection* by the aforementioned exercises, would not these exercises have ceased of course? But the same persons would fall again and again, and rise with the same transfigured countenance, and testify that they felt Christ in them, and were full of glory as before, and again cry out for Christ to come and pardon and save them from their sins; so that at every meeting the same sacrifices were continually offered; which was plain evidence that their affections were raised by an influential faith, *a confident expectation of* [39] *things hoped for, and the evidence of things not seen.* And if any should build upon their faith and deceive themselves with the *shadow,* and think it was the *substance,* they must blame themselves, for common sense is capable of making the distinction.

Obj. 4. But if it was the true light of the spirit they were in, must not that light have secured them from any such mistake? I answer, why did not the light on mount Tabor show the three disciples that what they saw was only a vision, and that Jesus was not yet glorified? Why were all the disciples so mistaken about the kingdom of Christ, both before and after their master was crucified? Why did they expect it to come with observation, and immediately appear? And why were they so mistaken as to think that John would never die? etc.

The light of God was never sent to those who were under no mistakes, but to such as were all over immersed in errors and mistakes, and willing to see it, and have their mistakes corrected. The first work of God is to discover errors and mistakes and have them put out of the way, and this must needs be done, before anything substantial and permanent can be built up. Hence the work among the *New Lights* was intended to tear down and remove the rubbish of old systems, and therefore the subjects of it, had practically and experimentally, to handle and prove the corrupt materials of the whole fabric. To be elected and singled out as the distinguished objects of irresistible grace, carried through the deplorable fall even to the resurrection, and after being raised up in glory, soul and body reunited, openly acknowledged and acquitted as dear children of God and made perfectly blessed, (as they had supposed) yet after all, they found they were in their sins, *"exposed to all the miseries in this life, to death itself, and to the pains of hell forever."*

Consequently the whole building must be one grand mistake throughout, and therefore in obedience to that light, by which they discovered the rottenness and danger of the old building, they determined to forsake it, or roll it piece by piece out of the way, until the way was prepared for a better foundation to be laid. The disciples and [40] followers of Jesus had his promise that they should receive the Holy Ghost, who would abide with them forever; that he and the Father would come and make their abode with them. But until the promise was fulfilled their old Pharisaical errors remained, and they were liable to pervert and abuse all the new light they received, by mixing it with their vain superstitions and traditions of men. The greater part gloried that such a Savior was raised up to Israel, but if they had not been mistaken they would rather have gloried in such a *breaker* being raised up to Israel. The disciples of Jesus were much more mistaken at first than his avowed enemies, for the latter evidently saw that he would be the occasion of taking away their place and nation, unless he could be defeated by superior power; whereas the former imagined that his whole design was to build them up. Hence in the midst of all their glorying, and the exercise of such spiritual power as they had, they were so often warned not to rest in what they had received.

No wonder then if many of the opposers of the late revival, in its first stages, were capable of forming a more correct judgment concerning the visible effects of it, than those who were in it, and of improving upon the admonitions given to the disciples of old in a similar case, to convince the *New Lights* that all their mighty gifts did not carry them out of the reach of danger. Not every one that saith Lord, Lord, For many will say unto me in that day, Lord, Lord, have we not prophesied in thy name, and in thy name cast out devils? And in thy name done many wonderful works? And then will I profess unto them, I never knew you: depart from me ye that work iniquity.

[41]
Chapter Four

Concerning the separation of those called New Lights from the Presbyterian Church.
Original Pages 41-72

A DIVISION must always precede a separation. That division in sentiment which began about the commencement of the present century in the Presbyterian church, continually increased until it effected an important separation, which took place in the month of September, 1803. A particular account of which is published in a Pamphlet, entitled *An Apology for renouncing the jurisdiction of the Synod of Kentucky,* printed in Lexington, (K.) 1804. It is an old proverb, that "two cannot walk together unless they be agreed." For nearly three years the subjects and promoters of the revival, continued their outward church membership with those whose constant labor it was to oppose and suppress it; this was a painful situation to both parties: for the *New Light* to be chained down in silence, forbidden to pray, exhort or make any noise or uproar in time of meeting, however clearly he saw the danger of the wicked, or felt his soul overflowing with the love and goodness of God. And no less painful did it feel to the expounder, and those who contented themselves with his learned and ingenious labors, to be interrupted by a sudden shout, and put to silence by the din which commonly followed; and worst of all, to hear that system by which he had all his wealth in this world, and the hope of a favorite interest in a better, set at naught by the general proclamation, *whosoever will, let him come and take of the water of life freely.* But thus it continued until the unequivocal and open testimony of several ministers, came forth in vindication of the new doctrine and the operations and exercises which attended it, and in pointed opposition to the Presbyterian system. This furnished the desirable occasion of banishing from the standing community, those flaming zealots whom ministerial authority had failed to reduce into subjection. [42]

II. But that those who were destined to excommunication on account of their faith and zeal, might not be wholly left without the usual claim of congenial descent from Leo the great, the dissenting ministers voluntarily withdrew from under the jurisdiction of the Presbyterian church, and according to their own history, "*constituted themselves into a Presbytery, as you will see from the minutes of their meeting.*" (See Apology, p. 37)

"We the above named Robert Marshall, John Dunlavy, Richard McNemar, Barton W. Stone, and John Thompson, having entered the above protest and withdrawn from under the jurisdiction of the Synod of Kentucky, and of the Presbyteries to which we belonged, do now formally unite in a body as a Presbytery, known by the name of the Presbytery of Springfield."

The design of these men as they themselves testify in all their writings, was not to lay the foundation of any church or distinct party, but as they express it (Apology, p. 20) they considered this:

"Presbytery providentially formed to cover the truth from the impending storm and check the lawless career of opposition."

Nevertheless they proceeded to organize what they called churches, although they considered their existence as only *pro tempore,* a kind of asylum for those who were cast out, that they might *come forth and be there* like David's father and mother with the king of Moab, *until they should know what God would do for them.*

III. On this occasion, as far as the way was opened for a separation, the subjects of the revival who were sincere in their profession, generally came forth and united with the seceding body, which were distinguished by the name of SCHISMATICS.

As this separation was productive of a very important change and placed the subjects of the revival in a different situation from what they had been, as far as it extended, it will be proper to trace the outlines of those new formed churches in their separate capacity, and the first thing to be considered is their manner of constituting. Every house must be built upon some foundation; all human creeds and confessions had been [43] disannulled or rolled out of the way; the power and authority of modern clergy, as successive to the apostles was renounced, and the Presbytery of Springfield confessed and denied not that they were as far off the true foundation as the rest. In this predicament they concluded that they would stand the safest and be most retired, and most out of sight from contending parties, upon the foundation of all their foundations, viz. the scriptures. The following minutes extracted from the records of the Turtle-Creek church will develop this point more particularly; according to which plan the churches in general which are called *Schismatic,* were organized:

April 20*th,* 1804. "The session taking into consideration the propriety of a more close attention to the government and discipline of the church, think it expedient to state to the people at large who have considered themselves under our care, the following observations on that subject."

I. "We think it the privilege of the church, mutually to profess their regard to the holy scriptures as the only rule of faith and practice, the only standard of doctrine and discipline."

II. "We think the eldership ought not to form a separate body distinct from the church itself, nor go out of doors secretly to transact such business as concerns the body of the people at large."

III. "We think it tends to keep the body of the people in the dark and obstruct a real spirit of communion, to examine and admit members, try causes of scandal, censure, rebuke, reprove or suspend in secret, or to transact privately by the representatives of the people, such or any other business of a public nature."

IV. "We think it expedient in order to the due exercise of government and discipline, that all who believe should be together in one place."

"We therefore recommend that the church constitute in the place for public worship," etc. "Moreover that the foregoing observations be publicly read in the congregation, and the voice of the church taken on the expediency of immediately reducing them to practice. Signed, William Bedel, Malcham Worley, Matthias Spinning, Aaron [44] Tullis, Samuel Sering, Francis Bedel, Richard McNemar. Accordingly at the close of public worship the above observations were read, and after a brief discussion of the subject, the following propositions were stated to the members of the church in particular, viz. Do we adopt the holy scriptures as the only rule of faith and practice, the only standard of doctrine and discipline? Do we agree to constitute a church, and in that capacity to transact business? The questions being put were answered in the affirmative with uplifted hands, without a dissenting voice. The number were about seventy-four who voted as above, remained in the house after the congregation was dismissed, and took their seats as members of the church. It was moved that the use of *(lead)* tokens be laid aside, and the members all take their seats at once. It was also moved and agreed, that the endearing and scripture appellation of brother and sister be revived among the members."

It is to be observed that in those congregations where the members of the new Presbytery resided, the Presbyterian mode of government had been practiced for some time after the separation. Neither did the Presbytery immediately resign their reputed authority, although in everything they introduced some alteration.

They considered it their prerogative to license public teachers, or rather to forward those who they believed were chosen and called of God. The following, written at Springfield, March, 1804, will serve as a specimen:

"Forasmuch as our brother, Malcham Worley, has made known to us the exercises of his mind for some time past, expressive of a divine call to labor in word and doctrine, and we being satisfied from a long and intimate acquaintance with him, of his talents both natural and acquired, being such, as through the grace of God, may render him useful; and considering that the way of God is above our ways, it therefore seemed good to us with one accord to encourage our brother to the work, whereunto we trust the Holy Ghost is calling him; and we do hereby recommend him to the churches [45] scattered abroad, to be forwarded in his calling according to the manifestation of the spirit given to him to profit withal. Signed in behalf of the Presbytery." B. W. STONE, *Clerk.*

As it was but a short time before the Presbytery were convicted that their union was formed upon antichristian principles, and under that conviction dissolved, it will be unnecessary to say anything further concerning the government and discipline exercised by them. Their principal object was to set the people at liberty from the contracted folds into which they had been gathered by idol shepherds in *the cloudy and dark day*. And as soon as they constituted into separate body as above, with the scriptures unexpounded as their only index, nothing remained for the Presbytery to do in relation to them, but to sit and watch as Jonah sat in his booth, to see *what would become of the city*.

It now remains to give a more particular account of the churches and people called *Schismatics*.

IV. From their own expressions it is difficult to say what their real character was in their own estimation.

They speak of themselves as *a church* about to constitute *a church*, but how the first was constituted appears not to have been considered. Again, they speak of the people *at large*, the churches *at large*, etc. If these expressions have any definite signification, they must mean the churches *at liberty*, the people *at liberty*, etc. To be set *at large* and *at liberty*, means one and the same thing. It follows then, that they considered the people who had been set at large by the preceding work, as now constituting churches *at large* or *at liberty*, who should be bound by no form of doctrine or discipline, but stand loose upon the variegated fields of antedeluvianism, patriarchism, Judaism, baptism, Christianity and Gentile-partyism, or whatever else was meted out between the lids of the bible, either by history, precept, promise, or prophecy. Yet notwithstanding this extensive liberty, it is truly marvelous and astonishing to consider the regular manner in which they proceeded from thing to thing in the investigation of truth. And what is still more striking, is the [46] union and harmony which existed among them in those investigations, and the subordination which they manifested in relation to those who were considered the most deeply initiated into the mysteries of the spirit. Taking what is called the *New Light* doctrine as the rudiments of divine

Chapter 4

truth, they proceeded to consider the nature of justification, reconciliation to God, etc. etc. concerning which I shall state a few particulars.

They rejected as a dangerous error, the doctrine of justification by the *imputed* righteousness of Christ, and taught that no one could be justified or accepted of God but that they forsook their sins and became *personally* righteous; that no one could be pronounced *just,* upon the principles of truth, who was not so in reality, and therefore when the true God accepts any as righteous in his sight, it must be such as are in reality so. Reconciliation or *atonement* is to be *at one* [united]*;* Christ is *at one* with God; we must be *at one* with Christ. God is unchangeably holy, just and good, and therefore cannot be reconciled or *at one* with an unholy, unjust and wicked sinner. Man in his natural state is unjust, unholy and wicked, therefore God and man in his natural state, are at *two,* not *at one.* Christ the mediator came into the world to *atone us to God,* not to reconcile or *atone God to us,* for if God is reconciled or *atoned* to man in his natural state, it must be becoming unholy, unjust and wicked, this cannot be. Therefore the work of reconciliation or *atonement* is to make man like God, holy, just and good, and for this purpose Christ came into the world. There is wrath and enmity to be taken out of the way; this wrath and enmity never was in God, for *God is love,* therefore it must be in man, and to remove it out of man the blood of Christ was shed, and to man that blood must be applied, not to the throne of God's justice which is unchangeably holy, just and good. Therefore Christ dying *for sin* was to *condemn* and *destroy it,* not in the *room* and *stead* of it that it might live. (See Stone's letters, p. 15 and 20.)

According to the *schismatic* doctrine, the vicarious sufferings of Jesus Christ in the *room* and *stead* of sinners that they might live, was only a cunningly devised [47] fable, destitute of foundation either in common sense and reason or the scriptures of truth, that proxy sufferings were inadmissible by any just law, either of God or man, as it would be wholly unreasonable and unlawful to hang a civil honest man in room and stead of a murderer, that the latter might be delivered out of the hands of justice and set at liberty. And according to the unchangeable law of God, *the soul that sinneth it shall die.* From whence it was plainly deduced that there could be no reconciliation or atonement to God, until the evil spirit, which is prone to evil, and that continually, was overcome and rooted out of God's creature, and as soon as that spirit which is opposed to the law was extinct, sin which is a transgression of the law, ceased of course, and the soul which came from God became reconciled and *at one* with him; and hence followed the necessity of the sufferings of Christ being commensurate to the atonement and glory that should follow. He sets us an example that *we should walk in his steps:* He suffered in the flesh that *we might arm ourselves with the same mind.* Thus Stone's letters on Atonement, p. 33 "It is evident that Christians according to their measure have fellowship in the sufferings of Christ, and are filling up that which is behind of his afflictions, in their body." Upon this principle it was evident that all who were in Christ *suffered with him,* that they might be glorified together, *witnessed the sufferings of Christ,* 1 Pet, v. 1. *rejoiced in his sufferings.* (ch. iv. 13.)

That when the glory should be revealed, they might be glad with exceeding joy. The sufferings of Christ abounded in Paul, which were effectual to the Corinthians; not to exempt *them* from sufferings, but in their *enduring the same sufferings which he also suffered.* (See 2 Cor. i. 5, 6.) But the greatest depth of the *schismatic* doctrine, lay in the reciprocal union which they supposed must exist between Jesus Christ and his followers, which rendered both the sufferings and glorification identical in each, and left no room for the disciple to suffer in the *room* and *stead* of his Lord, any more than for the Lord to suffer in the *room* and *stead* of the disciple; and therefore if the sufferings of Christ abounded in the [48] disciples of Jesus, the disciple did not suffer in the room and stead of Christ, but *very Christ* suffered in him the same as in his master. Hence they taught that all that were born of Christ and united to him, were *true Christ* as much as *fire* produced *by fire,* is very *fire* of *fire;* and as Christ proceeded from the Father, and was *true God* of the *true God,* so all that were born of the divine nature and seed of heaven, were *perfect in one.* Thus Stone in his reply p. 19:

"It is very evident that the seed of Abraham are all believers. These believers are one, therefore not called *seeds* but *seed.* For there is neither Jew nor Greek, there is neither bond nor free, there is neither male nor female; for ye are all one in Christ Jesus. Gal. iii. 28. For as the body is one and hath many members, and all the members of that one body being many, are *one body* so also is Christ. 1 Cor. xii. 12. Hence by *Christ,* in this verse, the Apostle means believers who are *in Christ.* And so I understand Gal. iii. 16. And to *thy seed,* which is Christ, i.e. to all believers."

See also Observations on Church Government, p. 14. Upon the strength of this article of faith, the *Schismatics* were so abundant in their profession of having *Christ in them* and being full of God, both the Father and the Son. Not that they held as an established principle that a real hypostatical union existed between them and God, but a hypothetical or supposed union depending upon their faith, as *all things are possible to him that believeth.* The *possibility* of standing in so near a relation to God, afforded a lively anticipation of it to the mind while in the full exercise of believing, but still left room for the following prayer:

> "Come, Father, Son and Holy Ghost,
> And seal me thine abode:
> Let all I am in thee be lost;
> Let all be lost in God."

Were a swine capable of believing that it was possible for him to be lost and swallowed up in man, and be incorporated with the human body and become one with it, the anticipation of such an exalted state might be very pleasing to the mind of that base animal; but [49] should he imagine that man would from the union by swallowing him alive just as he was, he must find himself greatly mistaken in the issue. Now considering the great disparity between sinful man and God, it need not be thought strange if those who express the above prayer with great fervor, should be as greatly disappointed when the process is entered upon, by which the all important union is affected. The *Schismatics* however, considered this union to have taken place first of all in the person of Jesus Christ. Hence many important questions were agitated concerning this extraordinary person, the end of his mission into the world, the nature of the work which was given him to do, and how that work is to effect us, etc. Upon which different hypotheses were formed according to the proficiency of each in the *New Light* and the *Schismatic spirit.*

V. It was agreed on all hands, that God was unchangeable and needed not the sufferings and death of his Son, to render him propitious to the soul of any; that it was through love that he sent his Son into the world, that sin is the only thing in the universe that he hates, that he would have all men saved from it, and that to effect this, Christ made his appearance in the world. But that *innocence* and *love* could not suffer and die in the room and stead of *guilt* and *enmity.* Nor could the imputation of innocence and purity to the guilty and vile, render them happy in the presence of heavenly beings of a contrary nature. From these premises it was concluded and taught by some, that man by departing from God, lost the true knowledge of his character and fell into a gross mistake, in concluding that he was their enemy; that Christ came to reveal the true character of God in order to convince sinners of their mistake, and prove to them that God was their friend; that he had sufficiently established this point by submitting to be killed by them, rather than oppose or hurt them.

Upon this hypothesis the Savior was supposed to die in the room and stead of the wicked, in a sense, somewhat different from the former. Inasmuch as the parties must meet, and the sinner looked upon God as his enemy, and was determined [50] either to kill or be killed; the love of Christ to the wicked was so great, that he chose to be killed rather than kill, and this was supposed to constitute *the gospel, the glad tidings,* viz. that although wicked sinners killed their best friend through a mistake yet he freely forgave them. When any believe this they repent and are reconciled to God as their friend, whom before they thought to be their enemy. This gospel method of salvation was however by no means established as a matter of common faith. The generality still believed mankind to be under deeper disorder, than such a mistake. For *after that they knew God, they glorified him not as God. And did not love to retain God in their knowledge.* Besides, if there is such implacable enmity between the sinner and God, that one or other must die, and if the enmity is found in the sinner, he must certainly be in the wrong; therefore unless the Deity sacrifice his law and justice as well as his life, out of love to the sinner, death and suffering must inevitably seize upon him that he is in the wrong.

Moreover if the sinner is at enmity against God whatever the cause be, if God is reconciled to him in that state, he must be at enmity against himself. Therefore upon this principle, should the sinner conclude that God was reconciled to him, had nothing against him, overlooked his enmity, disobedience, etc. the last error must be worse than the first. So that from the propositions first laid down, another conclusion was drawn more consistent and which was more universally embraced, viz. that the coming of Christ into the world was to make an end of sin, and unless we are wholly delivered from it, we can never see the face of God in peace.

VI. Pursuant to this conclusion, the first of those new satellites,[1] which the Presbytery of Springfield had recommended as a light to the churches, began to shine out in the month of June, 1804; and from the radiant splendor of the great luminary, around whose centre the *Schismatic* body revolved, proposed to obviate every difficulty that had been attached to those intricate subjects, and lay open the whole matter plain to the weakest capacity. But however plain and obvious the new divinity might have appeared to him or to others at the time it [51] was divulged, certain it is, that none but Schismatics, federalists or such as unequivocally maintain the sacred rights of conscience, could ever have admitted the opening of sentiments so singular, with impunity. But under the auspicious wings of the *American Eagle,* which shades the honest enquirer after truth from the burning rage of popes and despots, the reader may calmly peruse those singular propositions which were so generally ascribed to a disorder in the brain, in which the following ideas were included.

"Man was at first created in the nature and image of God, but being tempted and giving way to the serpent, the nature of the serpent was begotten in him, which is an earthly, sensual and devilish nature, directly opposed to the nature of God. This diabolical nature, however contrary to the *divine,* in which man was created, could not overcome nor extinguish it; hence there remained in the same person two opposite natures, at enmity and war the one against the other; the one designated *the seed of the woman,* the other *the seed of the serpent.*"

2. "Adam begat a son in his own likeness, *a double minded man,* and in this situation the whole human race were propagated, and thus they remained till Christ made his appearance and began the work of redemption."

3. "Jesus Christ the redeemer, assumed in the body of his flesh the same diabolical nature, which was in all other men, was made in all points like unto his brethren whom he came to redeem, had two distinct and opposite natures residing in his one body, of which the one was true God, the other very Devil. This diabolical nature which worked in the man, (and not some other being outwardly visible) tried and tempted him to seek temporal riches and honors, to convert the stones into bread, and cast himself down from the pinnacle of the temple, in order that *he himself* might be acknowledged and adored, as the coming Messiah. This wicked nature being denied of all its demands, crossed in all its cravings, gave him up for a season to the ministry of angels, but afterwards rallied its vanquished [52] powers, and struggled for life and victory against the Son of God, but was again overcome and held to the painful and ignominious cross, on which he was worn out, wasted and consumed as by a lingering fire, until he was forced in his last convulsive agonies, to cry aloud and yield up the invisible and immortal spirit. Thus the work of final redemption was finished, and the *second man* arose and ascended out of that lawless and wicked nature into which the *first* fell. Then the serpent's head got a finished bruising, and the first born of the woman's seed put everlastingly out of his reach. According to this transaction all the types, figures and allegories in the old testament, and parables in the new are to be understood. Thus, Cain and Abel, Ishmael and Isaac, Esau and Jacob, the sumptuous glutton and Lazarus the beggar, the foolish and wise virgins, etc. are to be considered as types of these two

distinct natures; the one elect, the other reprobate; the one beloved, the other hated; the one and his offering accepted, the other rejected."

"Again, the divine nature or seed of the woman which was chosen, redeemed, exalted and glorified in the person of Christ Jesus, is denominated in scripture *the spirit, the inner man, the new man,* etc. Its opposite, *the old man, the man of sin, the son of perdition, the flesh which lusteth against the spirit, the carnal mind, that wicked which sitteth in the temple of God* and defiles it: which in the work of redemption must lift up his eyes in torment, be punished with everlasting destruction from the presence of the Lord, be consumed and destroyed and go into final perdition."

"This *wicked* which is *one* and the same in all men, being overcame and destroyed in the person of Jesus Christ, laid a foundation for the gospel to be preached to every creature under heaven, and for all to look and hope for redemption at his final appearing.

That it was necessary that this gospel should be published to all the world, before a full end of that *wicked* should come. By this gospel he was bound, but suffered to live another day, or thousand years. This thousand years is now expired and the period come for that [53] man of sin to be finally consumed from off the face of the earth. And for this end, the spirit of God is poured out upon the people, first to reveal, and then to consume this *wicked.*" Such were the general propositions advanced by Malcham Worley, in the summer of 1804, and which was acceded to, by a number of those *Schismatics* who were considered foremost in the *New-Light.*

VII. An epitome of the foregoing doctrine may be seen in Stone's letters p. 23, 24. in which are the following expressions. *"From whom or from what did Christ redeem, etc."* I answer: 1st from the Devil. 2. He came also to redeem us *from sin,* which is the same as to redeem us from the Devil.

Mankind are represented as sold under *sin,* serving *sin,* servants to *sin,* under the dominion and reign of *sin,* etc. Hence it is plain that Christ redeems us *from sin* or from all iniquity."

"I now inquire what was the price given for our redemption? The blood or death of Christ is every where in scripture, declared to be the price given. Acts xx. 28. Rev. v. 9. etc. It may now be asked if Christ or God in Christ, redeems from the Devil and sin? And if he gave his blood as the ransom or price, who got the price? The Apostle to the Hebrews answers: *Forasmuch as the children were partakers of flesh and blood, he also himself likewise took part of the same, that through death he might destroy him that had the power of death, that is the Devil.* Here then we see that the devil had the power of death, and he got the price, which was the death of Christ. Then was fulfilled that old prophecy, *I will put enmity between thee and the woman, and between thy seed and her seed: It shall bruise thy head and thou shalt bruise his heel.* Gen. iii. 15." This particular point, "*the devil getting the price,*" was combated by Dr. Campbell, in his strictures: Whereupon br. Stone agreed "to eat these dreadful words" because so extremely offensive to the Doctor, and the occasion of a wildness of imagination in the Calvinist preachers and people. (See *Reply,* p. 55.) But neither Dr. Campbell nor br. Stone fully understood the expression when they agreed that it should be eaten. [54] The offence of the expressions seemed to lie in giving the devil something that was precious; hence the Doctor's objection, "*that the precious blood of Christ was given by God to the devil in payment!*" That "*God was so merciless as to deliver up his only Son to glut the malice of a blood-thirsty demon!*" That "*the lamb of God was immolated on the altar of hell,*" etc. But had he adverted to the Apostle's idea, quoted by Stone, viz. that this precious blood was intended to destroy the one to whom it was given, it must have appeared more consistent for the devil to get it, than the justice of God. The Doctor would not be so unreasonable as to give a dose of tartar emetic [poisonous salt] to one in perfect health to create bile on his stomach, and thereby *at-one* him to the bilious [acid, bile]. He knows the precious tartar emetic (which is the very essence of bile) must be deposited in the bilious bowels of his patient, in order to collect into union with itself everything there of its own nature and carry it off in the draught.

Now admitting that Christ assumed that blood, life or nature, in which all mankind lay separated from God, that life was his, and he had a right to do with it what he pleased, and although it was endowed with no greater excellence in him than in another considered in itself, yet it might be denominated *precious,* from the use which he made of it, and admitting that he gave it up as a public sacrifice, made a show of it openly and put away sin by the sacrifice of it, the Doctor must grant that Stone's inference that "the devil got the price," was not so full of horror as he at first imagined, and consequently it must prove a very strong emetic to him that eats it.

VIII. The above *schismatic* doctrine, as far as it was opened and explained, threatened the total subversion of the Calvinistic system at one blow; for upon the principle that sin must be actually destroyed, that Christ did actually assume, overcome and destroy it, and that the same battle must be fought, and the same victory gained by all who are born of God, it follows of course, that *proxy* sinning, suffering, obeying, dying, rising, reigning, etc. are the proper effects of a disordered [55] brain. And moreover if it was *the enmity* which Christ nailed to the cross and took out of the way, and the *Devil* which he destroyed by death, the hypostatical union of two distinct natures in the Son of God forever, must be a capital mistake, and all the worship that has been offered to him upon such a faith, must have conduced to the dignity and honor of *that spirit,* which the meek, lowly, and self-denying Savior foiled upon the mount. In fine, the

Chapter 4

Schismatics taking it for granted that sin was the whole occasion of *two*[2], That Christ came to destroy it, that his veracity was pledged to finish the work, and that the time of the promise was near at hand, expected, in whatever way the work should be affected, the day would soon declare it.

Several objections were raised in the *Schismatic* fraternity against brother Worley's manner of understanding the scriptures, the most particular of which was 1st: That it led to Universalism and made Christ the Savior of all men eventually, as well as officially; taking it for granted, that either in the plan of redemption or the execution of it, God had distinguished the souls of men by number and person. And 2nd. That if such a doctrine was established it would open a wider door to vice, inasmuch as it would cut off at once from the carnal mind, the powerful influence of hope and fear; consequently the wicked spirit in man would become more violent, and sin with more greediness, knowing that his time was short. But as all agreed that they were only yet beginning to learn the mysteries of the scripture and each one had a right to exercise his own faith, and walk by the same rule, and mind the same thing whereunto he had attained, the investigation of these mysterious and intricate points, was put off to a future period, and the churches went on harmoniously in the first principles of the *New Light* which they conceived to be so well established by the extraordinary power and gifts of the spirit. I shall now proceed to give some account of their particular form of government, manner of worship, etc.

IX. It has been before observed that they constituted by a vote, which considered the scripture as the only [56] written oracle through which the mind of God was revealed to them. And in order to this general suffrage, (in which the body of the people at large had equal privilege) every claim to superiority, (by a succession of church offices) had been laid aside, consequently the power of government was considered in the body of the people thus constituted. This new republic, under the standard of liberty and equality, and invested with so great a degree of light, life and power, assumed a threatening aspect toward the little surrounding kingdoms which had so long been weakening each other by civil broils. It is difficult to paint the zeal for liberty, and just indignation against the old aristocratic spirit, which glowed through every member of this new confederacy. And under the influence of this warm democratic zeal these churches soon exhibited an appearance, distinct from anything that had ever been seen. The following minutes of the church at Turtle-Creek will serve to illustrate some of the particulars of their proceedings.

"April 21, 1804. John Miller, Amos Valentine, and Joseph Stout, publicly related the circumstances of their conversion, with which the church was well satisfied and gave them the right hand of fellowship, as worthy members of the suffering body of Christ. Samuel Kimbel informed the church with tears, that he had wounded his own conscience and the cause of God, by associating with the wicked in a tavern, and tossing a dollar for whisky; professed his abhorrence of such conduct and his determination in future to be more guarded. The church was satisfied with his repentance and agreed that the offence be forgiven."

"J. F. informed the church that he had been overtaken in a quarrel, in which he suffered anger to rise in his breast, whereby the holy spirit was grieved. Yet as he did not manifest that the leaven was purged out, in such a manner as to feel the fellowship of that spirit which turns the other check to the smiter, loves an enemy, and returns blessing for cursing; the church agreed that he be kept on suspense till further satisfaction be obtained." [57]

Observe, it was upon the supposition that Christ was in this body of people, that transgressors came forward and confessed their sins, and such confessions were not considered as being made to men, but to God, and the forgiveness to proceed from that spirit, which was *at one* with the Father and the Son. In this mode of government, the republican body was filed off in a separate capacity, and the surrounding multitude were considered as belonging to a different family, and any one might have the privilege of coming over, confessing their wickedness, professing their repentance and uniting with *their spirit* as far as they chose. And the way was as free and open for any to change sides in a different manner. These churches still retained the use of the sacraments, but from the change which had taken place in the ministry, the end and use of the sacrament was very differently considered. When the imputed righteousness of Christ, the satisfaction made to justice in behalf of the sinner, and the imputed authority of the standing clergy to minister in the name of Christ, were set aside, the former use of the sacraments must of course go with the rest, for there remained no one regularly ordained to administer them.

It may be enquired whether these churches did not consider themselves authorized to ordain ministers. I answer they did not, as appears evident from the tenor of their faith on that subject, as stated in the *Observations on Church Government,* as well as from the manner in which they acted in relation to that important matter. The farthest that they went was to express their *satisfaction* with, and encourage those who they believed had power and authority given them from heaven, as appears from the following minute, dated "*Sept. 20, 1804. The church took into consideration the case of Brother Worley, relative to his laboring in the word, He was examined as to his soundness in the faith, with which examination the church was satisfied:*" and he was encouraged to exercise his talents in public exhortation, as providence might call and direct.

The *Schismatics* had too fresh a remembrance of the sufferings they had undergone in obtaining liberty from [58] the reputed vicegerents of Christ, acting in his room and stead, to allow them to lay hands suddenly on any one, and especially as they conceived it necessary that the Holy Ghost should be given in the important article of ordaining a true minister of the Gospel.

In consequence of encouragement from the republican body, there were certain individuals who took the lead in public exercises, which leads me to state some of the peculiarities of their worship.

X. From their general faith that God and Christ had their abode in the soul of man, and from those inward feelings of love and power which they occasionally felt, through the medium of a lively faith, they were led to believe that whatever exercise was congruous to that inward feeling, and had a tendency to increase it, was acceptable to God, as true worship. Hence by giving the right hand of fellowship to those who were admitted into the community, and finding that it tended to increase the inward workings of the spirit, it was gradually introduced as a common act of worship, in concert with singing hymns and spiritual songs. The whole society, old and young, male and female, would commonly unite in this mode of worship, and taking each other by the hand, would shake not only their hands but their whole bodies, like one churning, with such violence that the place would seem to quiver under them. This they called rejoicing, and in this worship they considered it the privilege of every one to unite who believed the new doctrine of atonement according to an observation of br. Stone, when he first heard that doctrine stated, viz. "that if these things were established as truth he would rejoice forever." Admitting that God was love, could not be changed, -was the same to one soul as another, would have all to be saved, etc. nothing remained but for the soul to love God and rejoice in confident hope of salvation, and manifest its faith and confidence by every such bodily exercise as had a loving or joyful appearance. The *New Lights* had considered it presumption to perform any of these bodily exercises voluntarily, into which they were forced by a supernatural power, but this [59] kind of faith appeared childish to the *Schismatics*. They supposed that whatever God moved the creature to by his irresistible power, must be acceptable to him. And therefore it was their privilege to do voluntarily what was acceptable to God, rather than be once in a while dragged to it, and the rest of their time offer up such voluntary worship, as was "full of unbelief and sin," and a stench in the nostrils of Jehovah.

The *New Lights,* struck down and held under the power of death for a time, then raised up as in a new world of light and vision, and carried away with such raptures of joy, could not possibly conceal their conversion. Such a conversion and way of manifesting it, however acceptable it might be to God, as being the effect of his irresistible power, yet the *Schismatics* conceived it to be more acceptable to God, (and not without good reason) for one who was convinced of sin and had turned from it, to rise up in the assembly of those who were like-minded, testify his views and feelings, and declare his intentions boldly and voluntarily. And again if he was overtaken with a fault, if it should be so small a thing as tossing a dollar for whisky or suffering a little anger to arise in his breast, that he voluntarily confess it in the open light and profess his abhorrence of it. There must appear a very marked difference between this worship and that in which the sinner was overtaken with the power of God, and constrained to do what he did not love, and might afterwards excuse himself that he could not help it, and still claim his union with the world by a voluntary profession that he was yet a sinner, prone to evil, no better than any other; and all that distinguished him from others, was the lighting down of a sovereign power upon him which he could not avoid.

The *Schismatics* conceived they were worshipping God to acceptance, while relating their conversion, expressing their abhorrence of sin, and singing spiritual songs to that effect, "*I shall be holy here*", shaking hands and shuddering with indignation against their soul-enemies, crying out for final deliverance from them. "*Make me Savior, what thou art: live thyself within my heart.*", Leaping and [60] skipping voluntarily in the joyful hope, "*Then the world shall always see, Christ the holy child in me.*" So that the principal thing that distinguished the *Schismatic* worship from that of the *New Lights,* was their taking the privilege of exhibiting by a bold faith, what others were moved to by a blind impulse. This they considered a great improvement, growth and advancement in the spirit of the revival: And upon this principle, the voluntary exercise of dancing was introduced as the worship of God, by br. Thompson and some others who were forward in promoting the grand *schism.*

Although this singular worship was practiced voluntarily with a degree of formality, yet it was not introduced in a formal way, but by following up and improving those operations which at first irresistibly forced them into that exercise. At the spring sacrament at Turtle-Creek in 1804, br. Thompson had been constrained just at the close of the meeting to go to dancing, and for an hour or more to dance in a regular manner round the stand, all the while repeating in a low tone of voice, "*This is the Holy Ghost, Glory!*" But it was not till the ensuing fall or beginning of the winter, that the *Schismatics* began to encourage one another *to praise God in the dance* and unite in that exercise; just believing that it was their privilege to rejoice before the Lord, and *go forth in the dances of them that make merry.*

However, notwithstanding the *Schismatics* aimed at that worship which should be expressive of uniform and continual joy, yet they were far from attaining it, and at least the one

Chapter 4 69

half of their exercises were of a contrary nature: some of a voluntary and others of an involuntary kind.

Among their voluntary acts of worship, were the general confession that they were sinners, rebuking, reproving, and laboring to reclaim their fellows who were more notoriously wicked than the rest, Some praying to God to *sanctify* their *corrupt natures,* etc. and others praying against their prayers. This kind of praying-match was a very common *schismatic* exercise. They considered it contrary to their federal constitution for one to attack another openly by any [61] supposed authority, and therefore they had recourse to the spirit, and by the brightest, boldest and loudest gift of prayer, the cause was commonly decided. In this way they generally settled their controversies of every kind. One would begin to preach or exhort, and if his doctrine was judged unsound or uninteresting, he would be presently matched with a prayer, and whichever collected the greatest warmth and manifested the most lively sensation of soul, gained the victory, and interested the general shout on that side.

But there were moreover in the *schismatic* worship, a species of exercises of an involuntary kind, which seemed to have been substituted by the Great Spirit, in the room of the falling, etc. which had been among the *New Lights.* The principal of these, were the *rolling exercise,* the *jerks,* and the *barks.*

1. The rolling exercise which consisted in being cast down in a violent manner, doubled with the head and feet together, and rolled over and over like a wheel, or stretched in a prostrate manner, turned swiftly over and over like a log. This was considered very debasing and mortifying, especially if the person was taken in this manner through the mud, and sullied therewith from head to foot.

2. Still more demeaning and mortifying were the *jerks.* Nothing in nature could better represent this strange and unaccountable operation, than for one to goad another, alter-

nately on every side, with a piece of red hot iron. The exercise commonly began in the head which would fly backward and forward, and from side to side, with a quick jolt, which the person would naturally labor to suppress, but in vain; and the more any one labored to stay himself and be sober, the more he staggered, and the more rapidly his twitches increased. He must necessarily go as he was stimulated, whether with a violent dash on the ground and bounce from place to place like a foot-ball, or hop around with head, limbs and trunk, twitching and jolting in every direction, as if they must inevitably fly asunder. And how such could escape without injury, was no small wonder to spectators.

By this strange operation the human frame was commonly so transformed and disfigured, [62] as to lose every trace of its natural appearance. Sometimes the head would be twitched right and left to a half round, with such velocity, that not a feature could be discovered, but the face appear as much behind as before. And in the quick progressive jerk, it would seem as if the person was transmuted into some other species of creature. Head dresses were of little account among the female jerkers. Even handkerchiefs bound tight round the head, would be flirted off almost with the first twitch, and the hair put into the utmost confusion, this was a very great inconvenience, to redress which, the generality were shorn, though directly contrary to their confession of faith. Such as were seized with the *jerks,* were wrested at once, not only from under their own government, but that of every one else, so that it was dangerous to attempt confining them, or touching them in any manner, to whatever danger they were exposed; yet few were hurt, except it were such as rebelled against the operation through willful and deliberate enmity, and refused to comply with the injunctions which it came to enforce.

3. The last possible grade of mortification seemed to be couched in the *barks,* which frequently accompanied the

jerks, nor were they the most mean and contemptible characters, who were the common victims of this disgracing operation, but persons who considered themselves in the foremost rank, possessed of the highest improvements of human nature; and yet in spite of all the efforts of nature, both men and women would be forced to impersonate that animal, whose name, appropriated to a human creature, is counted the most vulgar stigma [dog?, snake?]. Forced I say, for no argument but force, could induce any one of polite breeding, in a public company, to take the position of a canine beast, move about on all fours, growl, snap the teeth, and bark in so personating a manner, as to set the eyes and ears of the spectator at variance. It was commonly acknowledged by the subjects of these exercises, that they were laid upon them as a chastisement for disobedience, or a stimulus to incite them to some duty or exercise to which they felt opposed.

Hence it was very perceivable that the quickest [63] method to find release from the jerks and barks, was to engage in the voluntary dance; and such as refused, being inwardly moved thereto as their duty and privilege had to bear these afflicting operations from month to month, and from year to year, until they, wholly lost their original design, and were converted into a badge of honor, in the same manner as the first outward mark of human guilt. Although these strange convulsions served to overawe the heaven-daring spirits of the wicked, and stimulate the halting *Schismatic* to the performance of many duties disagreeable to the carnal mind, yet in all this, their design was not fully comprehended, something doubtful and awful, was thought to be figured out [played out] thereby, which would suddenly *fall with pain upon the head of the wicked;* and nothing was more calculated to excite such fearful apprehensions, than the expressions that were sometimes mixed with the *bow wow wow,* such as *every knee shall bow, and every tongue confess,* etc. at least these kind of exercises served to show that the foundation was not yet laid for unremitting joy, and that such as attached themselves to this people, must unite with them as a *body* destined to *suffer* with Christ, before they could reign with him.

But however great the sufferings of the *Schismatics,* from a sense of their own remaining depravity, the burden and weight of distress they bore for a lost world, the hatred, contempt, and persecuting rage of all around them, together with the spasmodic writhings of body with which they were so generally exercised; yet they were not a little alleviated by the many extraordinary signs and gifts of the spirit, through which they were encouraged to look for brighter days. Among these innumerable signs and gifts, may be ranked, *the spirit of prophecy*, being caught up or carried away in this spirit, and remaining for hours insensible of anything in nature, dreaming of dreams, seeing visions, hearing unspeakable words, the fragrant smell, and delightful singing in the breast.

This spirit of prophecy is particularly worthy of notice, which had its foundation in a peculiar kind of faith, and grew up under the special influence of visions, dreams, etc. The first thing was to [64] believe what God had promised, with an appropriating faith; cast anchor upon the thing promised though unseen, and hold the soul to the pursuit of it in defiance of all the tossing billows of unbelief. This faith, so contrary to the carnal heart, they concluded must be of God. It must be the spirit of Christ, or God working in the creature, both to will and to do.

What is the promise but the purpose of God? And what is the purpose of my soul (says the *Schismatic*) but to have the thing promised. Has God promised?, he cannot lie: Has he purposed?, he cannot alter. Therefore what his spirit leads me to I shall possess, as certain as God is stronger than the Devil. Upon this principle all were encouraged to believe the promise, and immediately set out in co-operation with the promiser; and in proportion to the strength of their faith, to predict the certain accomplishment of that purpose of God, which they felt within them.

Notwithstanding this faith furnished a very bold foundation for predicting what should come to pass, yet it was far from comprehending the whole of that evidence, upon which the *Schismatic* looked for the purpose and promise of God to be fulfilled. It was very common for them to be caught up or carried away by the same spirit of faith, and be shown in bright and heavenly visions, the indisputable reality of what they before contemplated in a simple belief. In those ecstasies some would seem to desert the body, and leave it for hours in a state almost or quite inanimate. Others in their transports, would seem to use their clay tenement as a kind of instrument, to sign out and represent to the spectators, what the active spirit saw in open vision, independent of any of its mean organs. Of these extraordinary visions, nothing can be communicated here beyond an imperfect hint, and whether they ever be correctly stated on paper is a matter of doubt. Their general import respected things that were darkly hinted at in the scriptures, and hard to be understood; such things as were especially to take place in the latter days. And hence notwithstanding they had adopted the scriptures under the notion of a confession of faith, [65] yet it was not immediately to the scriptures they applied for light, but to that transporting spirit which opened clearly to the mind, those mysterious things recorded in scripture, which the wisest men upon earth, without the spirit, could not understand. See the letter to Synod, published in Stone's Reply, p. 63, of which the following is an extract:

"We view Christ as the only centre of union, and love the only bond. Let us labor after this spirit, and when we obtain it, then we shall all be united in one body. * * * * * * * * [sic] Some are groaning for the wounds, of the Presbyterian cause; some for the Methodist; some for the

Baptist, etc. each believing that it is the cause of Christ for which they are groaning. And some are as heartily groaning for the wounds of the Christian cause, without respect to names or parties. If we should unite our groans and cries to the Father of our mercies, for the general release and the coming of the Lord's kingdom with power, God would hear and answer us. O let us unite in the common cause. * * * * * * * * Then will Zion shake herself from the dust, shine forth as the sun in his brightness, and be terrible as an army with banners. Then shall she be a cup of trembling to all the people round about her, and shake terribly the nations. Then shall that man of sin be destroyed, and righteousness shall flow down as a mighty stream. These things, dear brethren, are not vain imaginations, for God is now about to take the earth. Thy kingdom come. Even so come, Lord Jesus.

"Brethren, yours in the Lord.

>R. MARSHALL,
>J. DUNLAVY,
>B. W. STONE
>J. THOMPSON.

"Danville, October 18, 1804.
"*To the Moderator of the Synod of Kentucky.*"

In these sublime figures was couched the whole purport of the *schismatic* vision, viz. the coming of the Lord's kingdom with power. A *one body of people,* [66] united in Christ by the pure bond of love; the house, habitation or dome of the king of kings, in which the groanings of Presbyterians, Methodists, Baptists and Christians, for the wounds of their petty party, causes should not be heard. A Zion or pure gospel church, shaking herself from the dust, i. e. from everything unclean, all that belongs to the serpent and shining forth like the sun (i. e. Christ Jesus) in his brightness. Setting the people to tremble, and shaking terribly the nations. Consuming the man of sin, and opening a stream of everlasting righteousness upon the earth.

These were bold figures, and that they were just about to be substantiated, required something more than a vain imagination to evince.

Sleeping and waking, the whole topic with these *Schismatics* was the increasing work of God, and the blessed kingdom just about to appear, and each one contemplating it through some special dream or vision, in which they felt confident they had a particular revelation of the Lord's Christ. This was the kind of *manna* which they were daily gathering, and out of the infinite abundance that fell on the camp, it may not be improper to deposit a little of it in the pot. In some of these rapturous scenes, they professed to be carried clear out of the body, and to be favored with a particular interview with the spirits of their departed friends, and to see and learn their different allotments in the invisible world. Sometimes they mixed with great multitudes who had embraced religion in the past century, and were waiting for the new Jerusalem to appear, and the way to be opened into the holy city.

At other times they professed to see the holy city, in the bright and heavenly glory, and to hear the songs of the angelic host; and that attempting to join them in their music, occasioned the melodious sound in the breast; and that entering into the overshadowing cloud of such celestial witnesses, perfumed their whole soul and body with a peculiar fragrance, which rendered everything of a mortal fleshly nature, disagreeable and unsavory. This peculiar fragrance, which could not be found in anything upon [67] earth, but the subjects of these strange operations, seemed of all other things, to bring the heavenly state the nearest to the senses of these people.

Under the influence of this singular perfume, (which seemed to answer to the scripture notion of the smell of

Christ's garments from the ivory palaces, and all the powders of the merchant) they would swoon away sometimes three or four times in a day, recover, rise, and dance round with such spiritual and elevated springs, as might render it doubtful to the spectator, whether they properly belonged to the gross inhabitants of this globe, or to some other family of beings.

Besides these singular transports, they had another species of vision more universal, in which the sun, moon, stars, mountains, rivers, plains, vegetables, animals, and a thousand particular things and circumstances in nature, were used as emblems of things in the spiritual world, or kingdom of Christ. One has a night vision of two suns, another of three moons, another, wide awake sees a great platform of bright stars in the noon-day hemisphere. From these they descend to apparitions of strange things upon earth. (See the *Raleigh Register* of last September, concerning the multitude of Celestial Beings seen on the Chimney mountain, hovering round a great rock.) One discovers a certain spot of ground illuminated all over with the brightness of burning fire, and thousands of human creatures flocking into it from all quarters, and instantly purified from all the effects of a gross and fleshly nature.

Another sees the air crowded with birds of prey, commissioned to devour the flesh of every dead beast. Another sees a road marked out in the color of bright light, a thousand miles long, and stands with his sight intensely fixed upon it, until he discovers certain persons coming forth with good news from afar. Some in their visions were employed in crossing rivers, climbing mountains, finding treasures, fighting serpents, or more delightfully employed in eating the fruits of the tree of life, bathing in clear water, casting off old garments and putting on new. [68]

In a word, all nature seemed to be impregnated with a new and spiritual quality, which rendered every object and every transaction presented to the mind, whether sleeping or waking, susceptible of some signification which, respected the then present work.

These short sketches may serve to recognize the astonishing raptures in which the *Schismatics* were carried along in full expectation of the kingdom of Christ, but such was the unremitted flow of that spirit, which transmuted everything into a different appearance, that were it supposable that disembodied spirits could enter living men and women, it might be thought that every visionary, recorded either in sacred or profane history, had rendezvoused in the *Schismatics,* and borrowed their active powers to revise their endless train of types and figures. At least it was, no doubt with the greatest propriety, that these singular people appropriated to their day, the full and perfect accomplishment of the following prophecy of Joel. *I will pour out my spirit upon all flesh, and your sons and your daughters shall prophesy, and your young men shall see visions, and your old men shall dream dreams, and I will show wonders in heaven above, and signs in the earth beneath, blood and fire and vapors of smoke.* And to put it beyond all dispute that the work among the *Schismatics,* was that alluded to by the prophet, they generally supposed the extraordinary shower of blood fell out in the summer of 1804, about seven miles from Turtle-Creek meeting-house, traces of which are preserved unto this day.

Not that they considered the spirit of prophecy, their dreams and visions and other signs, as having anything in them to be depended upon for salvation. But as the merchant hangs out signals about his door, to direct the people where to come for merchandize so were the prophesier, the dreamer, the visionist, the sweet singer, and fragrant dancer, hung out to the view of the world, to show where God was about to open his everlasting kingdom of righteousness, peace and joy in the Holy Ghost. This kingdom was what the *Schismatics* were peculiarly bent for, and short of this they determined never to stop. About the latter end of the year 1804, there [69] were regular societies of these people in the state of Ohio: at Turtle-Creek, Eagle-Creek, Springfield, Orangedale, Salem, Beaver-Creek, Clear-Creek, etc. And in Kentucky; at Cabin-Creek, Flemingsburgh, Concord, Caneridge, Indian-Creek, Bethel, Paint-lick, Shawny-run, etc. besides an innumerable multitude dispersed among the people in Tennessee, N. Carolina, Virginia, and the western parts of Pennsylvania, who were exercised more or less with the same spirit. Praying, shouting, jerking, barking, or rolling; dreaming, prophesying, and looking as through a glass, at the infinite glories of mount Zion, just about to break open upon the world.

At least those who were foremost in the *schism,* expected beyond a doubt, that another summer would not roll by with any degree of the light, gifts and power of God, short of that which brings full and complete salvation from all sin. And in this expectation, (besides the common exercises of shaking hands and pledging themselves to each other by everything sacred, that they would persevere in the sin killing work unto the full feast of the lamb,) they practiced a mode of prayer which was as singular, as the situation in which they stood, and the faith by which they were actuated. According to their proper name of distinction they stood *separate* and *divided,* each one for one; and in this capacity, they offered up each their separate cries to God in one united harmony of sound, by which the doubtful footsteps of those who where in search of the meeting, might be directed sometimes to the distance of miles. Whatever this portentous concert might have addressed to God in the inner man, a sensible spectator with the slightest attention might have gathered the general import of their univocal prayer, from such language as the following:

"LORD GOD, ALMIGHTY! Thou hast promised unto us eternal life, and this life is in thy Son. Thou art no respecter of persons. Glory to thy name, we believe it is thy will that all should be saved and come to the knowledge of the truth. We venture upon thy promise, and roll our souls upon thy truth and faithfulness, as the rock of eternal ages. Thou has invited us to come to the waters, without money [70] and without price. We take thee at thy word. Heaven's King, you know that we are thirsty. We have long wandered in the dry sandy desert of sin; but glory to God, we believe there is an everlasting fountain opened, and our souls have already began to taste the blessed waters. But Lord, we are not satisfied. We want the fullness; and we believe thou hast given us the foretaste, not to disappoint us; but to encourage us to press on to the overflowing fountain: and short of that we mean not to stop. We want to bathe in the ocean of Redeeming love, and wash away the last, and least remains of a fallen nature. Jesus, Master, we want to be like thee; holy, as thou art holy, Without spot and blameless. Come, Lord, and finish thy work! Cut it short in righteousness. We doubt not, it is thy will, even our sanctification. Thy perfect will is all we want to know. O send by whom thou wilt send. Work by means of your own choosing: only supplant, root out, consume and destroy the man of sin, the son of perdition, and set our souls at perfect liberty from his iron bondage. Jesus, Lord, inscribe thy character on our every faculty. Make our bodies the fit temples of the Holy Ghost. Diffuse thy nature through all our active powers; and let every member be moved and actuated by the impulse divine."

Could language be invented more expressive of the near approach of the day of real, positive, and full redemption? It therefore remains to give some account of those important realities, to which the foregoing signs and wonders pointed, and for the entrance upon which, they served as a preparation.

"*Shout, Christians shout, the Lord is come!*
Prepare, prepare to make him room!

On earth he reigns, we feel him near,
The signs of glory now appear."

I shall close this part of the history with a hymn composed on this preparatory work, though not originally intended for publication. [71]

"The least in the kingdom of heaven is greater than he." John the Baptist

PART FIRST.
THE twenty-first of the third month, in eighteen hundred one,
The word of God came unto me, that word which came to John,
"My gospel is preparing for this benighted land,
"Go and proclaim the tidings, my kingdom is at hand.
"Those souls that want SALVATION, their groanings I have heard,
"But ere they can receive it, the way must be prepared.
"In the dim rays of star-light, a work must first be done,
"Before their tender eyes can endure the rising sun.
"Repent and be baptized, must be your solemn call,
"The tidings of salvation must be proclaimed to all.
"He that believes my messenger commissioned from above,
"That soul shall be baptized with my refreshing love.
"When persecutions rise, from the advocates of sin,
"Your pliant soul must yield, like a reed before the wind.
"You may be greatly shaken, but never yield to fear,
"Before the scene is ended, my kingdom shall appear."
This blessed word like fire, ran through my mortal clay;
The former earth and heaven seemed all to pass away:
And while the kingdom opened in visions most sublime,
My spirit was transported beyond the bounds of time.
Awaking from this rapture, salvation was my theme,
The multitude supposing I only told a dream;
But some at length believed the living truth of God,
And flaming with the spirit, they spread it all abroad.

Chapter 4

Soon as the fountain opened for souls to be baptized,
The land was in commotion, the people all surprised
In thousands they resorted unto this living pool,
And as they felt its virtue, each acted like a fool.
With joyful tears a-flowing, mixed with a solemn laugh,
They cry, "the day's approaching when God will burn the chaff!"
In the blest anticipation, to threshing they begin,
To make a separation between the soul and sin.
With prayer and exhortation, they make the forests roar,
And such loud strains of shouting were never heard before,
The stupid antichristians, were struck both blind and dumb,
With such loud supplications, LORD LET THY KINGDOM COME? [72]
The wicked persecutors, who dared the truth gainsay [deny, contradict],
Beneath the hand of justice, their breathless bodies lay;
Triumphant round their corpses, the joyful concerts sing,
"Hosanna to our Jesus we know he will be king!"
The kingdom was proclaimed in loud prophetic strains,
The joyful news received, with ten thousand loud amens!
With mighty signs and wonders, the work did still increase,
To show the blessed kingdom was RIGHTEOUSNESS and PEACE.

PART SECOND.

FIVE preachers formed a body, in eighteen hundred three,
From antichrist's false systems to set the people free:
His doctrine and his worship in pieces they did tear,
But ere the scene was ended these men became a snare.
As witnesses for Jesus, they labored night and day,
To convince the blinded Pharisees that Christ was on his way;
But souls bound for the kingdom did strangely turn aside,
And for a little season took these to be their guide.
The word of God came unto them in eighteen hundred four,
"Your work is now completed; you're called to do no more.
"My kingdom soon must enter, I cannot long delay;

"And in your present order, you're standing in my way."
These preachers took the warning, and all with one accord,
Agreed such institutions must fall before the Lord;
And wisely they consented to take their righteous doom,
To die and be dissolved, to make the Savior room.
In their LAST WILL AND TESTAMENT they published a decree,
For Christians in Ohio, Kentuck and Tennessee,
To meet the next October, and swell the solemn prayer,
"Thy kingdom come, Lord Jesus, thy kingdom enter here!"
The meeting was observed, the solemn prayer was made;
We waited for an answer, which was not long delayed;
The precious SEED of Canaan, long growing in the east,
Was planted in Ohio, ere the next April feast.
The long expected kingdom at length began to spring,
Which to many has appeared a strange mysterious thing;
But we'll trace it through that summer, the hottest scene of all,
And try to find its fruit in the next ensuing FALL. [73]
WHILE carnal antichristians, with their adulterous eyes,
Look out for some great monarch, descending through the skies,
The Savior's on mount Zion, our brethren and our kin,
Have brought that blessed gospel which saves us from all sin.
How foolish is this gospel to the aspiring Jew,
"What! call a man a Savior? O that will never do!"
But let their works be shaken out, before the gospel-fan;
Their souls will then bear witness, that Christ is in a man.
That full and free salvation, for which ten thousands prayed,
Is to the saints committed, just as the prophets said:
And all the honest hearted, will surely find it there,
While proud self-righteous hypocrites, eat back their feigned prayer.
That God that shook mount Sinai, and kindled such a blaze,
In Zion has his furnace, in these last burning days:
There honest souls confess their deeds, and every sin forsake,
And all the powers of darkness, their faith can never SHAKE.

[1] Malcham Worley. [2] *The expectants of Christ.*

Part 2: Chapter One

A
BRIEF ACCOUNT
OF THE ENTRANCE AND PROGRESS OF WHAT
THE WORLD CALLS
SHAKERISM,
AMONG THE SUBJECTS OF THE LATE REVIVAL
IN *OHIO* AND *KENTUCKY*.
Original Pages 73-86

THE *flesh lusts against the spirit, and the spirit against the flesh; and these are contrary the one to the other:* so that every person according to that principle by which he is governed, whether flesh or spirit, will conceive, judge of, and denominate things around him. And hence what is food and medicine to one man, may be poison to another; what one calls truth, another calls error; what is the work of God to one, appears the work of the devil to another; and even the heaven of one, may be another's hell. Thus the same thing is often distinguished by names directly opposite according to the sense of different persons. He who was called the Son of God by some, was designated by others, prince of the devils. And thus what one calls *Shakerism,* another calls *the testimony of Jesus Christ;* and a *shaker* in the language of some, is by others called *a true believer, a child of God, a follower of the lamb.* And what is still a greater contradiction, that which is called a work of redemption by some, others distinguish as a work of the deepest delusion.

From this diversity in the sense and language of mankind, it will be necessary to treat of this new religion [74] in a twofold order 1. According to the real sense, and understanding of those, who have embraced it. And 2. As it is addressed to the external senses of mankind in general.

In each part of the history, impartiality requires that I use the names of distinction and modes of expression peculiar to each. Accordingly I shall proceed in the first place, to give a brief account of the entrance and progress of *the testimony of Jesus Christ,* among the subjects of the late revival in Kentucky and Ohio.

Great expectations had been formed by the subjects of the revival, of something very great to take place in the summer of 1805. In which God would especially answer their ten thousand prayers, in delivering them from sin and opening the way into the holiest of all. Pursuant to which, the same spirit that had convinced them of sin, inspired them to pray, and confidently look for deliverance from it, and stirred up such warm expectations of its near approach. I say that same spirit on the first day of the first month, in the self same year, dispatched three men, viz. John Meacham, Benjamin S. Youngs, and Issachar Bates, from the Church at New-Lebanon, town of Canaan, in the state of New-York, with the testimony of Jesus Christ, and as *living witnesses* of God to open and confirm to the people, that way, and only way out of sin, that complete salvation which they themselves had found, and that everlasting life and glory, of which the Church in that place were in possession.

They arrived in Kentucky about the first of March, tarried a few days at Paint-lick, where they were kindly entertained; from thence they journeyed to Caneridge and spent a few days among the subjects of the revival in that place, among whom they were universally treated with unfeigned respect. From thence they passed over into Ohio and paid their first visit to Springfield, but without exercising any particular labors in any of those places; they prosecuted [followed to the end] their journey until they arrived at Turtle-Creek near Lebanon, on the 22nd of the same month. They came first to Malcham Worley's and tarried over night, and the next morning they came to my house, which was the first means by which [75] I knew that a church or people by such a name or description existed upon earth. We spent the remainder of the day principally in conversation on the most interesting points in religion, and from, all the evidence I could collect, I judged them to be men of honest principles, singular piety, and a deep understanding in the things of God, and as such I determined to treat them so long as their deportment was correspondent. Some of their conversation I could not so well understand; a number of things appeared new, but considering the copious field of truth too extensive for my comprehension, I was rather disposed to hear and learn more of God, than to shut out everything that was not included in my little sphere of knowledge.

The next day was the Sabbath, and as they desired to know whether the rules of our meeting would admit them to speak in public, provided they had a feeling so to do, I answered I knew of nothing to hinder. I was sensible [to] the spirit of the revival, as well as that of our wholesome government, imposed no restrictions on any man from testifying his faith, nor bound the conscience of any from hearing whoever they chose. And upon this principle, the door was fully opened for them to make any labors at Turtle-Creek, either in public or private to which they conceived they were commissioned. Accordingly Issachar and Benjamin attended the meeting and opened the testimony of Jesus to the congregation, which might all be summed up in this one saying, namely. *If any man will come after me, let him deny himself and take up his cross, and follow me. For whosoever will save his life shall lose it; and whosoever will lose his life for my sake shall find it.*

From their own feelings, as well as in behalf of the

Church from whence they came, they expressed great union with the work of God that had been for years past among the people, convicting them of their sins and pointing out by words, signs and particular sensations, the way and method of salvation; but they further testified that the time was now come for them to enter into actual possession of that salvation, of which they had received the promise, That the way to attain [76] it, was by self denial, taking up a full cross against the world, the flesh and all evil in our knowledge, and following Christ, walking as he walked, and being in all things conformed to him, as our pattern and head. Particularly according to St. Paul, *becoming dead with Christ to the rudiments of the world*, dying unto sin once, rising with him to a new, spiritual, and holy life, and ascending step by step in a spiritual travel, and separating farther and farther from the course of a corrupt and fallen nature, until we arrive at the perfect stature and measure of the sons of God.

That the first step in this saving work, was to confess all our sins, and when we confessed them, forsake them forever. And wherein we had injured and defrauded any one, to make restitution; in so doing we should find mercy; and being faithful, should receive that measure of the holy spirit, which would be an overcoming power, not only sufficient to keep us out of all actual sin and defilement, but to cleanse and purify both soul and body from the very nature of evil. These things they delivered, not as matters of mere speculation, but as things that had for many years been reduced to practice, and established by the living experience of hundreds in the church of Christ, to be the way and only way of God; the one door of hope for a lost soul, and the sure entrance into the righteous, peaceful and holy kingdom of God's dear Son.

They did not pretend to direct others a way which they themselves had not travelled, but testified that with these plain terms of the gospel, they had complied; and the substance of the promise they had received, and could say without boasting or dissembling, that they had received that overcoming power, which kept them faultless before the throne of God, even in the presence of his glory.

And moreover that it was a matter that greatly concerned us. That as Christ had now made his second and last appearance, for a final settlement with every soul of man, and as God had, wrought so great a work among us, in waking up, enlightening and preparing us to make a final choice; and by a special gift of his spirit, had sent us his lasting testimony [of] truth, we ought [77] to be very cautious how we treated it. For such as were illuminated in the great and marvelous light of the revival, to see the evil nature of sin, and stirred up to seek the way out of it, and had the last and only way of God opened to them, if they should reject it, their case must be deplorable. That although the light and power of the spirit might have been again and again restored to such as fell into sin, while they had not the proper means of keeping out of it, yet when those means were offered, should they be rejected, there remained no more protection for such a soul; but they must lose the salutary effects of their former light, and fall under the power of the wicked one. And upon this principle, that the subjects of the revival must either embrace the present call of God, and in obedience thereto, take up their cross and follow Christ, or gradually lose the extraordinary effusions of the spirit they had been under, and leaven back into a more corrupt and deplorable state than ever.

If a historian cannot be disinterested and unbiased, it is necessary that he be honest; and therefore I acknowledge that nothing ever presented itself to me, that so powerfully interested my feelings as the above testimony. And although I was not wholly unbiased, I can say with infinite propriety, I was far from being biased in its favor. A thousand objects presented themselves to bias me against it. But its intrinsic weight, the importance of the work that was past, the salvation of thousands that hung upon the point of its termination, and that of my own soul with the rest, balanced the weighty demands of the three insatiable idols of time,[2] and held me at least, upon an equilibrium for several weeks, so that without prepossession or predetermination, I could candidly investigate the subject, ready to go with the weight of evidence, where-ever it should preponderate.

During this interval, my searches and researches into the scriptures, their history, precepts, promises and prophecies, the signs of the times, my own past experience in religion for fifteen years, the nature of the past extraordinary work, [78] and the present state of the subjects of it, with all the rest of Christianity's professors, with the many questions and answers that passed in conversation, were they all written, would swell into a large volume. And in this kind of exercise I was not alone. The general agitation may be in some measure conceived of, from the following letter, dated Caneridge, April, 2, 1805:

"*My dear brother Richard,*
"I never longed to see any person so much, If I was not confined in this clay tabernacle, I should be in your embraces in less than an hour. The floods of earth and hell are let loose against us, but me in particular. I am seriously threatened with imprisonment, and stripes I expect to receive for the testimony of Jesus. Kentucky is turning upside down, The truth pervades in spite of man, Cumberland is sharing the same fate. The young preachers, some of them, will preach Jesus without the covering put on him by the fathers. The scribes, the disputers of this world, are gnashing upon us. Brother Matthew Houston has clean escaped the pollutions of this world, and he and his people are going on to perfect holiness in the fear of God. A few more will soon follow. Come over and help us is the cry made to us from every part. Brother Purviance is gone to Carolina to preach

the gospel there, by the request of some there. In a few weeks I start to fulfill a long daily string of appointments to Cumberland, by request I go, I have appointed two communions among many Christians on the heads of Little and Big Barrens. Brother Dooley is among the Cherokees again, His last rout [gathering] there was successful, some poor Indians received the gospel, He was solicited to return, He is truly an Apostle of the Gentiles, some few are getting religion amongst us."

"The churches thus, quid dicam? Nescio: [means] *What shall I say? I know not: my heart grieves within me. Certain men from afar whom you know, inject terror and doubt into many; and now religion begins to lament in the dust among us. Some as I suppose will cast away* [79] *the ordinances of Baptism, the Lord's Supper, etc. but not many as yet. Most dear Brother, inform me what you think of these men among us and you, from a distant region, Thank God he gave me his word.*{3} Letters show the substance and faith eats it. We all want to meet with you shortly: but by reason of my absence to Cumberland, Brother Purviance to N. Carolina, Brother Houston in Madison, we cannot meet on Turtle-Creek. Nor sooner than third Sabbath June, and that in Kentucky. Brothers Marshal and Houston parted from us yesterday. We administered the Lord's Supper at Caneridge the day before. Many communicants, much exercise."

"I am pushed for time to write to you. We have five students of the Bible, all but one know the languages, full of faith and of the Holy Ghost, just ready to preach. They all fled from the Presbyterians, to their grief, pain and hurt. Brother Stockwell exceeds expectation, and is beloved and useful. Our Apology is yet living and working, and tearing down Babylon in Virginia. It was re-printed there to the great injury of Presbyterianism. It is also re-printed in Georgia. We are just publishing a short tract on Atonement, I will send you one soon. This truth has unhinged the brazen gates

already, I am hurried, pray for me, farewell."
B. W. STONE.
"By friend Bates."

Great prospects were presented according to the above letter, on the part of the revival; the truth pervading and turning the whole country upside down. The Macedonian cry sounding from every part. The apology and tract on atonement, tearing down Babylon, or unhinging her brazen gates, some full of the Holy Ghost, just ready to preach, and one among them all who had clean escaped the pollutions of the world, and was going on to perfect holiness. But all this appeared unspeakably short of the glad tidings brought by the brethren from New-Lebanon, provided that what they testified concerning the church was true. It was well [80] enough for those who were in Babylon to cry for help, and for such as were appointed to the work, to tear her down and unhinge the brazen gates; but something beyond this must be taken into the account. We have news of a Zion, and what if her foundations are already laid. May it be that God has sent down the new Jerusalem for the refuge of souls, before he began to tear down the old buildings?

The Lebanon Brethren paid their first visit to Brother M. H. Perhaps he has believed and taken up his cross. How else can he have escaped the pollutions of the world? They have also been with Brother Stone, and opened the testimony there in part: perhaps he has taken hold of it, and means to make a final push for the kingdom through stripes and imprisonment. Or have these students of the Bible learned to appropriate scripture phrases to false and inferior objects. Brother S. and others may have received the name, *Holy Ghost* out of the Bible, but the thing must certainly dwell in the church. And admitting they are blazing full of the spirit, burning and shining lights, this goes no further than John the Baptist, it is far short of the kingdom of God. Those brethren from the east tell us that their people have got the kingdom, that they have attained it, by taking up the cross, and doing the works of Christ, and overcoming sin by faithful and diligent combat, that they are of God, and do not commit sin: but walk even as Christ walked, and are righteous even as he is righteous.[4] And moreover that he that commits sin, whatever his profession or gifts may be, he is yet of the devil. These things inject terror and doubt into many. John was full of the Holy Ghost, and for his testimony concerning Jesus, he was actually cast into prison, full of terror and doubt, whether this was he that should come or whether he should look for some other.

In fine, I could see nothing in the past work as a foundation to build upon. And what these strange brethren testified, appeared plain scriptural truth, and presented a way entirely safe for those who were able to receive it, and whether they were the people or not, [81] who had actually attained this salvation, it was very evident they were far before us in light and understanding concerning the way; and it was no doubt the will of God that those who desired to be saved should walk in it. Thus in the midst of reasonings, doubtful disputations and close examinations, the testimony was investigated at Turtle-Creek publicly and from house to house until it obtained the full credit of a number who had been leading characters in the revival.

Malcham Worley was the first who embraced it, opened his mind and took up his cross. With this I confess I was at first staggered, from a deep rooted prejudice that I had imbibed against some of his peculiar sentiments; but finally concluded that if Malcham had been more wild in his former exercises than the rest, he certainly needed salvation the more; besides it appeared that his conflicts with the man of sin, the son of perdition (as he expressed it) must shortly have terminated his existence upon earth,[5] had not his expected deliverer come out of Zion to turn away ungodliness from Jacob. But I was not a little surprised, that these strange brethren should come directly there, and he receive them with such cordiality, when I was well assured that no previous acquaintance had existed between them. This, with many other singular circumstances that occurred, restrained me from attempting to judge the mysterious work of God's spirit, but rather labor to get a deeper and more practical acquaintance with it. Soon after [82] Malcham set out in the narrow way, he was followed by a number, so that within three or four weeks from the first opening of the testimony, it had pervaded ten or twelve families. And from that period continued gradually to increase, so that at Turtle-Creek, the number of families which now stand in the faith of Christ's second appearance, may be stated between thirty and forty.

I shall now consider the entrance and progress of the testimony more particularly, as it respects the individual who receives it. The first point of faith in relation to the testimony, is to believe, that he who bears it is a *true messenger* and *witness* of Christ, in whom the spirit of truth continually abides; and that whatever instruction, reproof or counsel is ministered by such, it comes from Christ, who speaks *in him.* Therefore all who are taught in this manner are strictly and properly *taught of God,* and in obeying what they are taught they yield obedience *to Christ.*

Upon this ground the believer has to make a final settlement with an old systematic idea, that the spirit of God speaks invariably in the scriptures. Upon an impartial examination he finds that all the contradictory spirits among the professors of Christianity [religious sects], speak in the scriptures, and even the devil himself can speak in the scriptures; so that the scriptures are as liable to be spoken by an evil spirit as the good. It then remains to follow that spirit which goes as contrary to sin, and manifests its purity by its fruit, according to the scriptures, and the inward test of conscience. This is the spirit of Christ, and it sets them immediately to work to do the righteous will of God. And first of all to confess before God what they have done contrary to his will and the light of their own conscience. In this work, the honest believer might as well try to cover or conceal the most chafing mote in his eye, as try to hide or conceal anything which be has committed, contrary to the pure doctrine of the scriptures, and the holy example of Jesus Christ, of which he stands convicted by the witness of the spirit in his own conscience.

And here he has to combat the spirits of wicked men, who pretend [83] to speak in the scriptures, and say that it is idolatry to confess sin in the presence of man, and that God is to be found any where, in the fields, on the hills or under the green trees, and there we ought to make our confession in secret. But by following the spirit of truth, he overcomes this wild pagan error, and discovers, that according to the scriptures, God never accepted a confession of sin, which was not either made to those whom he had set in order in the church, or at least with the face toward that temple which was typical of his last habitation, viz. man. But the greatest evidence the true Believer receives, of this being the order and institution of heaven, is the divine light which he receives in consequence. Light by which sin appears more than ever hateful, and by which he is inspired with a growing zeal to roll out of his heart and practice the last remains of it; and lastly by which he discovers with increasing brightness the succeeding footsteps of true gospel obedience. To the sense of those who in the faith of Christ, have cleared their conscience from the deep rooted stains of sin, and received his spirit as their ruling principle of life, sin is so exceeding sinful, so hateful and pernicious that I am bold to say they cannot commit it.[6]

But he that is begotten with the divine nature of the Son of God, keeps himself in the element and works of that nature; so that he can no more commit sin than a fish can fly through the air, or an eagle dive to the bottom of the sea. But that abiding fervor and power of spirit which overcomes every motion of evil, belongs not to the entrance of the testimony, but a degree of progress in it. And this degree all must attain who come into it, or fall off as withered branches, for there remains no more room for either imputing their sins to Christ, or to a deceitful heart, or anything else by which they can be excused; but the soul that sins must bear its own iniquity, and burn under it without any mitigation or covering.

With an inward sense of the power, protection and presence of God, the Believer travels out of the use of shadows and signs, ceremonies and forms of worship, to which he might have been strongly bigoted while in [84] bondage under the law. There is no more occasion for calling upon God afar off, when he has taken possession of his body and lives and walks in him, nor of calling to his memory a departed Savior, by signs and shadows of his dying love, when the only Savior that ever redeemed a lost soul, is formed and living in him, and executing every branch of his office. Water applied to the body appears a beggarly element, compared with the baptism of the spirit. And as one baptism is sufficient to purify the conscience, he takes that and travels away from the superfluous shadow. Bodily exercises, dreams, visions and ecstasies, which had but a momentary effect on the blind and obdurate heart, and furnished at best, but a fleeting joy, gradually give place to the sun of righteousness, that shines continually the same, without cloud or eclipse. Hence in the progressive work of the testimony, a blessed reality, an enduring antitype is wrought in the Believer, which fully answers to all that he could possibly have conceived of, while longing, praying and hoping for the kingdom to come.

As Believers become more and more leavened into the nature of Christ, they discover with increasing accuracy, the latent corruptions of a fleshly nature, and the secret wiles of Satan in injecting his poison into the heart. And as they discover, so by the cross they overcome and gain an increasing victory over that which is death to the soul, by dying to it, the spirit of the testimony runs through all the Believer's behavior in public, in private and in secret, so that in no circumstance is he released from the work of self denial, or at liberty to defile his conscience with any act of injustice or uncleanness, contrary to the spirit of the divine law, or the nature of the Son of God who first fulfilled it. To the unclean lust of the flesh, in which the sinful selfish nature of man is formed, the followers of Christ stand in a peculiar manner opposed, and count it their distinguishing privilege to preserve their bodies in sanctification and honor. In the death of *that* in which all men by nature are held, they find deliverance from every branch of evil; such as pride, covetousness, anger, hatred, etc. so that by crucifying the flesh, its affections and lusts [85] wither of course, and they grow into a peaceable, gentle, kind and loving spirit, in which they can live together from one year's end to another, without feeling a hard thought, much less expressing a hard word one against another. And in such a spirit and behavior as cements them together in one fellow feeling, and promotes the peace, purity and happiness of the whole, the progress of the testimony mainly consists.

Moreover all who receive the testimony in the spirit of it, are taught thereby to be diligent and faithful in things temporal as well as spiritual, and to serve God with body and substance, as well as with their spirits. Hence the testimony has a proportionate progress in the frugality and honest industry of Believers, whereby they lay up in store a good foundation, not for their own pleasure and aggrandizement but for the honor of God, and the relief and succor of him that need.

By faith in the testimony, and the influence of that spirit

which accompanies it, without any other stimulus, Believers at Turtle-Creek began with confessing their sins, forsaking them and taking up their cross, and by the same faith and spirit, they came together on the 23rd of the fifth month, received one common gift, united in one common worship, and without murmuring or caviling [frivolous objection], have continued in it, increasing in love and union, peace, joy and harmony and every good word and work, unto the present day; and by this, I am emboldened to testify that the kingdom so much prayed for, is come according to the promise of God, and the order which divine wisdom laid out; and the saints have begun to possess that enduring substance, which prophets and kings desired to see and died without the sight.

The same faith produced by the preparatory work of God, began also to break out at Eagle-Creek sometime in the sixth month; which gave occasion to the testimony being opened there. A few at first embraced it with full purpose of soul, as the only way of God. In the month following brother Dunlavy stepped into the ignominious path and began to preach the faith, which for a time he had labored to destroy; and from thence forward the same work, worship, and [86] spiritual travel, went forward there as at Turtle-Creek, and exists at present in twenty or thirty families in the bounds of the meeting. Through the faith and special light of Matthew Houston, Samuel Henry, John Bonta, Elisha Thomas, etc.

The testimony entered and was received on the south side of Kentucky about the middle of the eighth month, and continued to spread until it embraced as many as were willing to embrace it, in Mercer, Shelby, Paint-lick, and Long-lick. In each of which places there are a number of families, who have denied ungodliness and worldly lusts, taken up their cross, live together in the unity of the spirit and bond of peace, and while with open eyes they are travelling from death into life, they shine as lights in the world. A few families at Beaver-Creek set out in obedience to the testimony in the spring of 1806, who were numbered with the faithful. The testimony is one and the same, wherever it is ministered. Is received into one and the same honest and good heart, and wherever it springs up and bears fruit to perfection, that fruit is one and the same. And that lawless and disobedient nature of the first man, which never did bring forth fruit unto God, they can jointly address without pity or compassion in the following language:

Awhile you may cavil and fret,
And think that the cross is too hard,
But now you must take what you get,
For death is your certain reward.

In Adam the second, I trust,
My beautified spirit shall find
A body that's free from all lust,
And pure as the heaven born mind.

{1} I call it *new religion* because that term is readily appropriated by all, and especially as those who are in possession of it, consider it A N E W C R E A T I O N, T H E N E W A N D L I V I N G W A Y, which makes all things new that come into it. [73]

{2} See 1 John ii. 16. [77]

{3} This Italic was originally in latin. [79]

{4} See 1 John, ii. 6. and iii. 7. [80]

{5} It was necessary that a work which promised redemption from sin, should include a perfect revelation of the whole root and foundation of it. And as the subject of this revelation, God made choice of M A L C H A M W O R L E Y; who, notwithstanding he was a man of unspotted character, of an independent fortune, and a liberal education; yet, neither his learning, his estate, nor his good name, could have saved him from total distraction, and the wildest convulsions of despair, when he came to behold in the open light of divine revelation, the whole depth of human depravity. Nothing but the miraculous power of God, could have supported him through such a scene, and kept him alive in the cheerful hope of deliverance, amidst the violent conflicts of an inbred nature, and the outward rage of blind and superstitious professors. [81]

{6} See 1 John iii. 9. and v. 18. [83]

[87]
Part 2: Chapter Two

SHAKERISM,

AMONG THE SUBJECTS OF THE LATE REVIVAL IN *OHIO* AND *KENTUCKY*.
Original Pages 87-105

HAVING given a short account of the entrance and progress of this new religion, according to the sense of those who have embraced it, I shall proceed to exhibit it in a more external point of view, in which I shall consider some of the errors with which it was branded, and the unreasonable treatment which it received on that account from some. Not that I wish to inspire the reader with the least degree of resentment against those who may have taken up the matter in a false light, and through a misguided zeal, acted an unreasonable and unlawful part in opposing it. Confident I am that if *Shakerism* was properly understood, there is no man in his senses could persecute it. Nor do I suppose that the religion of Christ, under any name, would ever have been persecuted by the men of this world, but through the instigation of a wrong-headed clergy. The government of Christ has nothing to do with the government of this world, and can therefore offer the citizens of this world no provocation. But through the false insinuations of those who have wished to incorporate the church with the world, and sit at the helm of civil and ecclesiastical affairs in conjunction; those who have marked and kept up the distinction, have been represented as the enemies of mankind, and treated as such.

Now if it is true that none of the princes of this world knew Christ Jesus, otherwise they would not have crucified him, what conduct might be expected towards those who walk in his meek and lowly footsteps, from the enlightened sons of Columbia, provided their judgment was not warped and twisted by that wild and voracious beast, which long ago made war with the lamb, and overcame him. Herod and Pontius Pilate would never have molested the harmless Jesus, but for the false accusations of the priests and high pretenders to religion, instant with loud voices crying, "*Away with him, He says he is the Son of God! He makes himself equal with God! He said he would destroy our temple, and build it again in three days! Away with* [88] *him! away with him! If you let the deceiver go, you will not be a friend to Caesar.*" It was not the peaceable citizens of the Roman government that characterized him a blasphemer, a malefactor, wine-drinker, and a whore-master, but those who professed to have all one father, even God.

And it was the same characters that pursued the saints as "*pestilent fellows, movers of sedition,*" enemies to the commonwealth, etc. wore out the patience of the civil magistrate with their clamors, and finally interested the secular arm to extirpate them from the earth. These things were written for our learning, that when we see any people persecuted for their religion, we may know it is not primarily by the commonwealth, but by the instigation of some ecclesiastical judge, and of course it is not really the religion itself that is persecuted, but something in the room of it, which the false judge has the assurance to palm upon the multitude while he demands their credit to his false coloring. That *Shakerism* has been grossly misrepresented in many instances, very few will pretend to doubt; and the source from whence these misrepresentations arose, must be peculiarly worthy of notice.

It is easy to perceive that the spirit of the revival had a peculiar tendency to put down that ministerial authority by which creeds and parties were supported, and set the people at liberty, each to follow the dictates of his own conscience. Upon this principle, the jurisdiction of the Synod of Kentucky was renounced, and the Presbytery of Springfield resigned their supposed authority. But though *Dagon fell before the ark,* yet *the Philistines set him again in his place.* The generality of the members of Presbytery, notwithstanding their professed resignation, continued in the full possession of their reputed authority; and in that capacity stood ready to judge of any increasing light that might be manifested, whether they were able to comprehend it or not.

Having shook off their former reins of government, and having attained but little mortification of that pride natural to man, and being carried along in a high gale of the spirit, they began to form great imaginations of an universal kingdom, in which they would fill the first rank. And as the ground work of this vast [89] kingdom, which must include the whole earth, they proposed to seize upon the sacred name, CHRISTIAN, exclusive of all other names; and so draw into union and one grand communion, all who wished to be called by that worthy name.

The plan of this great kingdom was drawn up by Rice Haggard, and published in the year 1804; which proposed as the leading foundation principles, simply to *worship one God*, acknowledge one Savior, Jesus Christ, have one confession of faith, and let that be the Bible, one form of discipline and government, and this to be the New-Testament, be members of one church, etc. (See Address to the different religious societies, on the sacred import of the Christian name, p. 21.) These high imaginations served for a season to amuse the people, but their eccentricity from the leading light of the revival, is easily perceived, by a little attention to the "*Observations on Church Government.*"

While the work of God continued in any degree of purity, it was not a *sacred name* the subjects of it were in quest of, nor was it the communion and fellowship of the millions who assumed the worthy name of Christ, that they sought: It was *the power of God unto salvation,* and that living spirit of Christ in the heart, by which they might grow into a holy temple in the Lord. But a scheme of human imagination, which proposed to organize all the denominations into *one great body of Christ,* was very suitable wherewith to confront a little testimony, which simply encouraged souls that were seeking salvation, to confess and forsake their sins and set out to follow Christ, in a life of new obedience. And therefore for the distorted features of *Shakerism*, the erroneous sentiments and wicked practices of those called *Shakers,* mankind in general are indebted to those, who by way of eminence are called *Christians.*

In perusing an account of this distinguished profession in *Browne's Western Calendar,* written at Springfield, August 26, 1806; the following sentence particularly attracted my attention, viz.

"They are not so vain as to think that all their thoughts, words and actions have always been exactly right; and they will thank any, [90] who in the spirit of meekness, will point out to them wherein they may be wrong, that they may amend."

This concession and request from one of the first ministers in this new *Christian* society, in behalf of the people in general, although I conceive it furnishes me with no authority to accuse them with ought, yet in reason, it must prevent their taking offence, should they know that a number of their words and actions are recorded in a spirit of meekness, which are conceived to be essentially wrong.

When the testimony was opened at Turtle-Creek, what

was spoken by the Lebanon brethren themselves, could not reasonably be condemned by those who heard it. But others at a distance, tossing about with the wind of imagination, and conjecturing things that had no reality, imbibed a spirit of prejudice against this doctrine of the cross; and especially as it bore an unfavorable aspect toward the great body of Christ which they had in contemplation. And therefore, the first words which I conceive were not *exactly right,* came forward in a letter from Springfield, dated April 5, 1805, a few of which words were as follows:

"It matters not to me who they are, who are the devil's tools whether men or angels, good men or bad. In the strength of God I mean not to spare. I used leniency once to the devil, because he came in a good man, viz. Worley. But my God respects no man's person. I would they were even cut off who trouble you. I mean in the name and strength of God to lift his rod of almighty truth against the viper," etc.

Now admitting that these were the wickedest men on earth, I am far from thinking that such menacing words, from one unprovoked could be justified; and how much less when on the same sheet, this concession appears,

"I do not say that they are not good men, or that the body of their sect are not such; perhaps they have more light than any other sect; perhaps they have had more power."

Where then could be the propriety of crushing them, or cutting them off, even upon the generous *Christian* plan of a coalition of sects.

In a foregoing letter it was complained that through faith in the testimony, the ordinances of Baptism, the [91] Lord's Supper, etc. were likely to be cast away. And in the epistle from which I have just been quoting, are the following words:

"These men have turned the gospel into a law of commandments contained in ordinances.",

Now from these two *Christian ministers,* who could learn the true account? Their words could not be both *exactly right,* for they stood in pointed contradiction. But further, considering that brother Thompson in the same letter acknowledged that he was far behind, not only in the light and liberty of the revival, but on every important subject, I conceive it was not exactly right for him to form such hasty resolutions to combat the testimony, even before he had properly heard it; and with that resolution, to come up to the camp meeting at Turtle-Creek, on the 27th of April, raise a sudden and passionate outcry against these peaceable men, assume the authority of leading the meeting, enter upon a public investigation of their doctrines, and in the close of it, pronounce with a loud voice, *they are liars! they are liars! they are liars! According to the fable, "A liar is not to be believed even when he speaks the truth."*

Therefore although it was readily granted, that these men spoke the truth, yet there remained this pretext for not believing them, namely, that they were declared to be liars; and upon this principle it was, that they were debarred by many from speaking at all in public. A man may be under an error, or he may be mistaken, and yet merit some degree of respect from his fellow-creatures; but a willful liar, a deliberate teller of lies, who can away with. Therefore under this opprobrious character, a bold *Christian* could cry to Issachar Bates, "Go to Hell," and while a wicked man followed John Meacham from place to place, spitting in his face, and crying aloud to *make a great fire and burn these false prophets,* some of the foremost who professed the worthy name, *Christian,* were at his back, laughing and encouraging him on. This and such like treatment, appeared so far from being *exactly right* among a people who aimed at monopolizing the name of Christ, that I am confident similar treatment from the wildest savages towards any men of civil behavior, must have merited severe reflection. [92]

At a succeeding meeting at Salem, the 11th of May following, I have no doubt but brother Thompson may have justly reflected, that he was not *exactly right* in debarring from the privilege of speaking, one whom he had long acknowledged his equal, and his guide; excluding all who believed the testimony, from any further communion or fellowship with the *Christians,* and especially as it was in pointed contradiction to their general *Christian plan.* "*Let none be excommunicated but for a breach of the divine law.*" (See Haggard's plan before mentioned.) Setting his own prejudiced spirit to speak in scriptures, as if it was the spirit of God.

And thus asserting, that the Holy Ghost had made him overseer of the flock, and that these *Shakers* were false Christs, false prophets, wolves in sheep's clothing, deceitful workers, transforming themselves into the Apostles of Christ, creeping into houses and leading captive silly women, dumb dogs, and every hateful name and character which the scripture could furnish. In consequence of which, they were railed upon by the *Christians* under these names wherever they went, and henceforward these members of "*the great body of Christ,*" conceived they had good authority from the word of God, to impeach them with everything that was erroneous, wicked and base, and not only palm upon them every filthy character named in the scriptures, but treat them as they supposed such characters deserved. Now if it was not *exactly right* to take the private interpretation of John Thompson on those occasions, and upon the strength of that, refuse any personal acquaintance with these men, it will follow that all the rough treatment they received in consequence, was *exactly wrong.*

I further conclude it was *exactly wrong* for my kind

brother Stone, after inviting me by letter to attend the general meeting at Concord the second Sabbath in August, to forbid me to speak on the occasion, or even to come to his house, and by a council of the *Christian clergy,* to impose upon brother Dunlavy, Benjamin Youngs and Malcham Worley, the injunction of total silence through the whole of the meeting, and (at the same time that many were soliciting us with tears to preach, and we thus pointedly [93] forbidden on pain of being prosecuted as disturbers of the meeting) to propagate among the people that we were the dumb dogs spoken of in scripture; (with which title we were often taunted.) On the last day of the meeting, six of the *Christian brethren,* viz. J. Thompson, R. Marshal, B. W. Stone, D. Purviance, J. Stockwell and A. Brannon, alternately delivered each his opinion of the *Shakers* in an address, in which some of them were named out, pronounced liars, defamed by many slanderous reports which they could have proved false, had they been allowed to speak.

Now if such treatment was *right,* the spirit of the revival, which allowed every man liberty of conscience, must have been wrong. But as I conceive it to be right for every man to hear and believe whoever he pleases, the above conduct appears not only subversive of the liberty of conscience so warmly contended for a little while before by the same brethren, but of the very spirit of a free government. For be it observed, that in all those places the people were anxious to hear the *Shakers,* and considered themselves as much related to those who were forbidden to speak, as to them who forbade them; until by the din of false reports and misrepresentations of their faith and practice, they were frightened into a spirit of prejudice.

Brother Stone, in the introduction to his Letters on Atonement, observes that the arguments used by his opponents, are "bold unscriptural assertions, hard names, delusion, error, doctrines of devils, Arminianism, Socinianism , Deism, etc. Such arguments (say he) have no effect on a candid mind, but they powerfully influence dupes and bigots. The candid look for truth and plain unequivocal arguments.",

Who then could he suppose, would be influenced by the following statement in the postscript of his reply to Campbell's strictures?,

"You have heard no doubt before this time, of the lamentable departure of two of our preachers, and a few of their hearers from the true gospel, into wild enthusiasm, or *Shakerism*. They have made ship-wreck of faith, and turned aside to an old woman's fables, who broached them in New-England about twenty-five years ago. These wolves in sheep's clothing have smelt us from afar, and have [94] come to tear rend and devour," etc.

If bold unscriptural assertions, hard names, etc. are wrong, I presume brother Stone's postscript is not *exactly right*. What plain unequivocal argument was ever advanced to prove that the conduct of these men, in a single instance answered to such a bold assertion. When Benjamin Youngs was forbidden to speak at Concord, by R. Marshal and B. W. Stone, the only reply he made was, "I am sorry to see you abusing your own light."

Now when to these innumerable hard speeches, are added, their inviting these strangers to their houses, stopping them at the door when they came, and forbidding them to enter, or at other times ordering them from their houses and laying them under the necessity of seeking their lodging among the weeds, and by such acts of inhumanity as a Deist would be ashamed of, encouraging a spirit of persecution; I think the *Christians* may well acknowledge, that all their thoughts, words and actions, have not always been *exactly right.* What but the example of this latest genus of Christians, could have instigated any part of a free and friendly republic, to beset the houses of the *Shakers* in the night, assault their persons with clubs and stones, break their windows, and burn their place of worship, throw down their fences, and turn in beasts to destroy their grain, cut and tear to pieces their apple-trees, crop and disfigure their horses, beat and abuse some of their bodies, and by every kind of mockery, railing and cursing, pushing, collaring and threatening, disturb and molest them in their worship.

Did the citizens of Ohio and Kentucky, know of a truth, that it was the meek and humble followers of Jesus Christ, that they were treating in this manner? Nay verily, but a people as they supposed of the most corrupt and mischievous principles. And as I apprehend the general statement which the *Christians* gave of their principles, was not *exactly right,* I shall mark out some of those mistakes. The first rough lineaments of *Shakerism* portrayed on the public mind, were, that it went to disannul [cancel] and cast away the Bible, to set up the word of man in room of it, to deny Jesus Christ, the resurrection and final judgment, to throw away the gospel and seek salvation by the works of the [95] law, etc. That these *Shakers* were enemies to the revival and came to destroy it. That their scheme was to get people's land and property, by parting man and wife, ruining and breaking up families. That they actually forbade to marry, and commanded to abstain from meats, and therefore without hesitation, they were seducing spirits, and their doctrine that of devils.

This general draught, laid a foundation for great improvement, both upon their principles and practice. And the *Christian minister,* who set the example of characterizing from his own private studies, without any personal acquaintance, had soon abundance of followers who felt entirely at liberty to publish anything which a fruitful imagination was capable of composing, and from this source it was, that the public generally received their information. And according as the wind of fancy blew, so it was a fact, credible at least among the *Christians,* that the *Shakers* castrated all their males, and consequently exposed their necks to the gallows, or divested of all modesty, stripped and danced naked in their night meetings, blew out the candles and went into a promiscuous debauch. And what was still more shocking, the fruits of their unlawful embraces, they concealed by the horrid crime of murder. In one instance, a prosecution was proposed against an individual, but the evidence, even for a suspicion, was so extremely vague, that the bill was handed back by the foreman of the grand jury, with a just reproof to the presenter. Such reports and conjectures, (of which there was an infinite variety) were generally taken upon the authority that Mr. *Such-a-one* heard a man say, that he saw a woman, who had it from a very respectable man, who saw the person who saw it. But in some instances, persons said to be of great respectability, would affirm (whether they meant with their natural eyes or the eyes of imagination) that *they themselves* saw such things. For such liberty brother Thompson, no doubt, laid a foundation in the following sentence of his letter of April 5.

"I see the mark of the beast on that church as plain as I see this paper while I write, and I know that I see it by the light of God."

In the light of the same god, I doubt not but ten thousand beastly actions have [96] been seen among this people; not one of which, the *Christians,* and all the world to help them, are able to prove, after sending out spies and watching their houses by day and night.

It has ever been foreign from the feelings of the Believers, to counter-plead such vague insinuations. They believe that God has called them to another work, in the progress of which, the truth will show itself without any strife of words. But as a number of things of considerable weight have been stated by way of objection, which have been maintained with some show of argument, I shall briefly investigate some of those particulars, merely to show the difference of sense and understanding on those subjects according to the evidence on both sides.

And 1. The *Christian minister,* after forbidding the Shakers to speak or the people to hear them, roundly asserts: *"These men say that we are in a new dispensation. That Christ is come the second time, and the resurrection and final judgment begun."* The young believer would reply, "Very well: A new dispensation is what every enlightened soul has been looking for and the coming of Christ is that for which ten thousands have been praying; and he must now be somewhere on earth, as the scriptures are true. For the time is up, according to Daniel, John, and all the prophets, for the sanctuary to be cleansed, and the power of the holy people restored, the authority of antichrist taken away, and the saints to possess the kingdom. And what other resurrection is there to life, but to come out of that state of sin into which the *first Adam* fell, and come into Christ the *second Adam* who is *the resurrection and the life?*

The matter we now animate and which is constantly upon the change, we are not to expect after its dissolution, to be again subtracted from the elements of this globe and repossessed in its primitive form, at the expense of every other body with which it may have been incorporated. And what other final judgment are we to expect, but simply and honestly, in the presence of God, and Christ, and before the saints who are appointed to judge the world, confess all that we have ever done amiss, repair our wrongs, set out to forsake every evil, and [97] grow up into Christ, as the infant grows into a man? *There is a natural body, and there is a spiritual body;* the former belongs to the fall, the latter to the resurrection. Therefore it is not old skulls and rotten flesh that are to be raised up in glory, but that spiritual body of which we are called to be members; which is already raised up by the power of God, and ascending into the heaven of heavens, far out of sight from this lost world.

Obj. 2. "These men say that each one of them is a Christ, and we must throw away our Bibles, and follow them."

Ans. This statement is not *exactly right.* They testify that there is but one Christ, whose footsteps they follow, and though they are by nature no better than other men, yet in following Christ they may be safely followed according to the scriptures.

If three honest republicans, in order to reclaim a band of tories, should invite them to become their followers even as *they* followed Geo. Washington or Thomas Jefferson, would this furnish a sufficient reason for stating that each of these men professed to be a Thomas Jefferson? and therefore they must be liars, there being only one man in America of that name. Or if these Tories had a copy of the United States' Laws, which they abused, would it be proper for them to say that the honest citizens wanted them to throw away their law book, because they would have them to live according to these laws? With no less impropriety were the *Shakers* charged with professing to be each a Christ, and requiring the Christians to throw away their Bibles.

The subjects of the revival, had unanimously believed that Christ would make his abode and appear in man, and that it was their privilege to believe and follow the truth delivered by man, according to that measure in which it was opened and revealed. This was certainly the faith of brother Thompson himself, when in the spirit of the revival, as appears from the following expression, in a letter, dated April 22, 1803:

"The Lord may have made known to one, what another

is ignorant of. I bless God that he has made you capable to teach me in the things of God."

And even in his [98] letter of April 5, 1805, he has so much remaining candor as to say,

"God in mercy visited your soul with light while I remained in darkness, He sent you to this country with the light to sow it here, and made you the instrument of bringing the heavenly fire to Springfield, where my soul caught the flame of this revival. Ever since that time you are in my heart to live and die with you."

Now if it was the faith and order of the revival, to follow the truth of God testified by man, it could not be *exactly right* for any to pretend that they were going on in the spirit of the revival, and at the same time laboring to destroy all confidence in every living teacher. Crying out-

"Don't believe man, don't follow him, you need not believe us, for we may and do err, you must just take the word of God and read that, There you have the truth, and you may believe and practice it, precisely as expressed in the words of scripture."

Yet the people were shut up to the necessity of believing *some body,* and rather than believe those who had been called liars by others, they gave credit to the opposite character, who asserted concerning *themselves* that they were *not to be believed* and in obedience to that faith, learned first to call the Bible by a name which it never gave itself; and according to that name, practice whatever was commanded or even permitted in scripture words; assured that God immediately spoke to them in that scripture, even though it might have been originally spoken by a Pharisee, Sadducee or devil.

Although I have heard the abettors of the *common Christian cause,* maintain that Gen. iii. 4. *Ye shall not surely die,* and Mat. iv. 6, 9. *If thou be the Son of God, If thou wilt fall down and worship me, etc.* were the words of God, and to be taken. without any explanation; yet I have supposed it was rather to avoid the force of truth, which they were unwilling to acknowledge. However in nothing short of this could the general principle find any consistent basis, and the implicit believer of bible words, must learn his duty from the following sentences as directly as any others. *Rejoice O young man in thy youth, walk in the ways of your heart, and in the sight* [99] *of your eyes, Go take unto thee a wife of whoredoms, Drink thou also and let thy foreskin be uncovered, Drink ye and be drunken, and spew, and fall, and rise no more, etc.*

Obj. 3. "They say we must be saved by the works of the law, Their doctrine leads into bondage."

Ans. They believe that outward circumcision, with every other Jewish ceremony, which the Apostles called works of the law, were abrogated by Christ, nor have they attempted to revive any of them. But Christ in disannulling these dead works, made no provision for *bad works.* The only alternative he left for any, was to follow him in the regeneration, or continue under the law and under its curse.[1] This doctrine never proposed anything but bondage to the Jew, who expected to be pardoned for *Abraham's sake,* and accepted on account of his clean outside. Now such an objection as made no distinction between *good* works, *dead* works, and *bad* works, came very improperly from those who contended so warmly for liberty to continue in sin, as well as in the use of those works, which they themselves acknowledge, were adopted in the room of circumcision and the Passover.

Obj. 4. "They forbid to marry, and attach criminality to that for which we have the express command of God."

Ans. This I am bold to say every Believer in Kentucky and Ohio, have from the beginning contradicted. Forbidding anything implies authority, and attaching criminality to anything, belongs to a law. Now these men never proposed any other than the law of Moses, and every man's conscience as a criterion to distinguish between good and evil. Therefore what was thus already condemned, did not remain for them to criminalize. And upon the generous principle, that every free agent ought to be allowed in matters of religion, to act according to is own faith, they have never to my knowledge, imposed any prohibition on an individual in relation to matrimony. It is true, that *for the kingdom of heaven's sake* they choose to be even as Christ, in that respect. But their receiving a particular saying of Christ, and living precisely up to it, claims no authority over [100] the children of this world; they have an indisputable right, according to their own laws, to marry; and every church may adopt such laws and forms of matrimony as they think proper and with any such laws or forms, the *Shakers* have never interfered.

The *Christians* have labored hard to establish the above objection, and not without some plausible pretext. And had the witnesses against Christ no pretext for asserting, "We heard this fellow say, I will destroy the temple of God?" Did he not say, *"Destroy this temple"* and *"I will"*? And where was the great evil of transposing the words and putting *"I will"* before *"destroy,"* when it was so essentially necessary to condemn the deceiver? But I suppose it would be granted, even by the false witness himself, that he was not *exactly right.* Again, according to their testimony, he was no friend to Caesar. Why? Did he not pay his taxes? True, but he would not fight, he would rather turn the other cheek to the smiter; and spoke of another kingdom. If then Christ was plausibly and unjustly accused with aiming to destroy the Jewish temple, and supplant the empire of Caesar, so were the *Shakers* with the above.

It was in fact the *Christians* who assumed the authority on the occasion, and set out to enforce a law given to man in a state of innocence, for the fulfillment of which he wholly unfitted himself by the fall. Gen. i. 28. That law or command as it respected fallen man, the *Shakers* supposed the Son of God had disannulled [canceled, done away with], and from it they conceived they were redeemed by Christ, as well as from all outward ceremonies of atonement, that fallen man had ever lain under in consequence of his disobedience; and in claiming this right of redemption, they had enough to do to answer the objections of their accusers, without entering any accusation against others.

And although in disannulling the commandment going before (by which sin took occasion to work in human nature all manner of concupiscence [strong desire]) they violated no existing law, either of God or man, (except what St. Paul calls *a law in the members, a law of sin and death.* Rom. vii.) Yet upon the authority of these *Christian ministers,* they have been publicly [101] condemned as the blackest of criminals, and treated according to that character, as far as the wholesome laws of our state would dispense with. Then how far must it appear from being *right,* for those who claimed the sole power of judging, and whose judgment was not only sanctioned by the shouts of the multitude, but in many instances severely executed, to represent as their unjust accusers, those who were judged, condemned and punished according to *their law*.

Obj. 5. "The testimony of these men go to part man and wife, and even encourage men to beat and abuse their wives, and turn them away."

Ans. How can that be parted which is one? Did not God say, "they twain shall be one flesh?" These men have more understanding than to propose a separation of this kind. And therefore the testimony they bear, takes no notice of man and wife, It came from that world where *they neither marry nor are given in marriage, but are as the Angels of God.* The testimony cannot be chargeable with evils to which it may indirectly give occasion, any more than the proclamation of American Independence is chargeable with all the acts of outrage and cruelty, perpetrated by the British during the revolutionary war; and therefore that some of the *Christian brethren,* have taken occasion from the testimony to beat and abuse a sister, a wife, and drive her off, is matter of fact. But to charge anything of the kind to the *Shakers,* is *exactly wrong.* For although according to St. Paul, there is neither male nor female among them, yet I am bold to say that since Adam fell, woman never was treated by man with tender kindness and respect, superior to what is commonly manifested among the *Believers.*

Obj. 6. "They are a set of worldly-minded, cunning deceivers, whose religion is earthly, sensual and devilish."

Ans. These are the words of brother Stone in his letter of July, 1806. And the proof of this objection was the *fama clamosa.*[2] "The *Shakers* are come to take people's land, Every one that joins them must immediately give up his deed to the elders!" The *Christians* [102] were considered as very near to the *Shakers* in their doctrine and worship, is one reason why manythings may have been imputed to the latter, which properly belonged to the former. Some *Christian* fathers, who had the general title of land vested in them, in which others had a lawful partnership, refused to give separate titles according to their promise, but dispossessed their former brethren by profession and nearest kindred in nature, from their valuable and lawful possessions, merely on account of their faith. Moreover, the *Christian* church at Paintlick, refused to make a title to brother Houston for land which he had lawfully paid for, merely on account of his faith. But so foreign from this has been the conduct of the *Shakers,* that upon land which they purchased and paid for, mainly for the relief and benefit of others, not less than eight families are commodiously settled.

This I mention distinct from the daily stream of beneficence that flows from their threshold, for which they receive nothing in return but love and thanks, much less the unlawful surrender of a deed. Who then is the worldly-minded, cunning deceiver?

Obj. 7. "They prophesied that such as rejected the testimony would lose their former life and power:

"But (says Brother Stone in his letter of July) now the work of God goes on in spite of all the Calvinists, Shakers, and devils in hell. Now we know your prophets are liars."

Ans. The work of God never did go on in *spite*, but in love and kindness to all men, even the Calvinists not excepted. But while the *Christians* upon the slightest evidence of the *Shakers* being liars, can fall to shouting and praising their God, or at the sight of them, stop every medium of information with loud cries for deliverance, a work of some kind will no doubt go on in *spite* of everything that claims any relation to the coming of Christ. But how long God may trouble these mighty waters, and what degree of power may operate round about in that preparatory work, has never been predicted.

As I conceive much credit has been given to the boasted power among the *Christians,* upon the test of [103] the Shakers being liars, I shall mention one more particular upon which the testimony has been condemned as false. Lastly,

"These men have testified they would never die, and one of them from New-Lebanon has died already in despair, convinced of the delusion."

Ans. They never asserted that they would live forever, in the earthly house of this tabernacle. But that every true follower of Christ, has passed from death unto everlasting life, is a truth.

And even though brother Thompson had seen Prudence Farrington, dying at Turtle-Creek, under a deep conviction of the delusion, as plain as he once saw the mark of the beast on the Church to which she belongs, and should affirm that his vision was in the light of God, yet his vision I should pronounce false, and contradict his news of congratulation to his *Christian* brethren. And moreover, I should think it proper for any person who had taken any part in spreading such a report, to "eat the dreadful words." So tenacious am I of reasonable evidence.

I was among the last that conversed with sister Prudence before her departure from the body, and though I treasured up the most of her solemn words, and particularly the last, which were, "Strengthen the brethren," yet I shall only insert at this time a short extract of a poem composed on the occasion, to which I shall add, an extract of a letter to New-Lebanon, from which the contrast will appear. ,

EXTRACTS.

"HER holy example's of infinite price;
Brought up in the gospel, a stranger to vice,
Her cross from the first she did faithfully bear,
And finished her course in her thirty-first year:
Her heaven-born spirit, to angels akin,
(Not stained with the flesh nor polluted with sin,)
Has now got released from the sorrows of earth,
And shares the full joys of her heavenly birth."

"Our precious sister, Prudence Farrington, has finished her course, and is buried under an oak in the [104] wilderness of Ohio. She deceased the eleventh inst. [April, 1807.] in the thirty-first year of her age. A loving sister, a blessed virgin, a holy woman, an heir of glory."—

"She lived without sin, and died without fear;
She's not as she's been, and yet the is here"[3], I. B.

In fine, there is nothing pertaining to the testimony, but has admitted of objection, false statement and vague report. But it has not been my design to notice anything but what has been stated with some plausibility.

Next to the new and old doctrine of the cross, the hue-and-cry was raised against the new and old manner of worship.

"What! go forth in the dance? Go voluntarily without being jerked? And say they are praising God in the dance! The dances, also, of them that make merry, of them that serve the devil! Take their dances to serve God! Christians, read your Bibles, and you will see that these fellows are not of God, for they keep not the Sabbath." "Think" (says brother Stone, in his letter of July) "Think seriously and soberly of the shocking conduct of your reveling mock-worship, and tremble."

Could he have forgotten, that a little while before, when censured by Dr. Tod, a brother professor, for the same shocking conduct, his reply was, "that he had to move heaven-ward with him hanging at his heels." Then think seriously and soberly, what is a Tod at the heels of a traveler, in comparison of a Stone, a great stone?

"O my Richard (adds Barton) shall I ever rejoice over you as a penitent prodigal?"

Now (replies Richard) if ever: I have just returned from feeding the swine, confessed my sins, been completely stripped and clad with a suit completely new. The door has been opened into my Father's house, and I have entered, to go out no more. -Now the family begins to be merry, and the elder son to wonder what it means, willing to get news from the meanest scullion [male kitchen servant]. Don't you hear that it is MUSIC [105] and DANCING? And is not the Father entreating you to come in? Then,

> Brother cast your anger off,
> And every passion bury;
> Come in and share the fatted calf,
> And let us all be merry.
>
> Will you grieve about a kid,
> When the calf is killed?
> If you come in when you are bid,
> You may yet be filled.

⁽¹⁾ See Gal. iii. 10.
⁽²⁾ Noisy report.
⁽³⁾ Near the spot to which Brother Stone would have flew in April, 1805, had it not been for his earthly tabernacle.

Part 2: Chapter Three

SHAKERISM,
AMONG THE SUBJECTS OF THE LATE REVIVAL IN *OHIO* AND *KENTUCKY*.
Original Pages 105-108

A FEW REFLECTIONS.

WE live in what is called *The United States of America. United States!* A name that promises peace and happiness to every citizen; but, under this specious name of Union, what a picture is exhibited? A great Christian empire, divided into a thousand little kingdoms, all enclosed in the bowels of a great republic, and each contending for the mastery. America exulting in her health, the liberty and equality of her members, and yet full of worms, biting and devouring one another, each pursuing a distinct cause to which he presumes all others must finally give way. The Presbyterian minister, the Baptist, Methodist, Christian and Church minister, each proposing to reduce the whole commonwealth under his laws and government. In the midst of these party attachments, who shall be governor, representative, magistrate, major, captain, etc.? This question at once proves the spirit of the union, while it arouses Christian against Christian, party against party, each to contend with his fellow professor, who shall be the greatest, Tell it not in Great-Britain! Publish it not in the streets of London! Lest the daughters of Babylon sneer at the apparent effects of civil and religious liberty.

Whence arises this motley mixture of kingdoms and states? Is it not through a grand mistake, converting the Bible into a civil law-book,{1} and accounting those to rule who adopt it as such? From this egregious error, has not every aspiring worm been encouraged to form his separate party, set himself at the head of it, read and [106] expound his laws, bestow privileges and execute judgment upon his subjects? And can it be otherwise until the eye of common sense is open to see that the kingdom of Christ has nothing to do with civil government, and that civil government has nothing to do with the church or kingdom of Christ? Let this plain maxim of Christ be adopted; of course that civil institution about which there has been such an uproar among the Christians of late, will be restored to where it belongs.

II. That the abusers of the Bible have betrayed great ignorance and idolatry in assuming the reins of government by the supposed authority of that book, and given great occasion of disgust to the name of Christ, is a truth that every man of good sense will yet acknowledge. Look at the Church common prayer book, established by a mighty defender of the faith, and it will appear that the subject of that kingdom, must either go unmarried or repeat after his priest the following obligations to a woman:

"With this ring I thee wed, with my body I thee worship, and with all my worldly goods I thee endow: In the name of the Father, and of the Son, and of the Holy Ghost. Amen."

"Come back! Come back," says the *Christian!* Where? "To the Church, the *one Church.*" Nay, let me rather be a Hottentot, and worship the moon, and have the liberty of giving part of my goods to the poor.

The *Christians* say, "let us all worship one God," then let them settle the point who it shall be. They say the word of God (i.e. the Bible) tells them so and so. Very well; it says, "*Fall down and worship me.*" This will not do. I dare not worship a book, and my soul recoils at the idea of worshipping that *spirit* which originally suggested these words. Therefore, I must worship according to my present faith, though it should appear "solemn mockery," in the eyes of all the Christian world.

III. I am thankful to the disposer of all human events, that I was not more than seven years old when the American eagle first stretched her pinions and began her ascent toward the air of liberty. And, therefore, the meridian of my temporal life is at a period when reputed fools and fanatics no longer smoke on the altar of [107] *Christianity,* but every man's religion may be correctly examined of whatsoever kind it is. Surely, if Church officers knew they might as well be still and silent, as to try to crowd back and shut up their flocks and cry, Wolves! Wolves! For every man's character must be known in this day, and each one judged not by his good words and fair speeches, but according to his WORKS.

IV. For upwards of two years I have studied *Shakerism,* with as close application as I ever bestowed on the system of Calvin, and at least upon as proper a plan. I have had the documents of it open before me without covering or disguise, i. e. the people who have set but to be righteous and follow Christ, in deed and in truth. And in all their actions at home and abroad, however scrutinized as a test of that faith upon which my salvation was suspended, I never have discovered anything that could furnish any ground of a trivial objection; but am bound to say, that the same characteristics of a child of God, which the *Christian* reads in his Bible, I have been able to read in the daily deportment of this people, and that without a blot. A people *blameless and harmless, without rebuke in the midst of a crooked and perverse nation among whom they shine as lights in the world, having their conversation honest,* and yet all manner of evil spoken against them falsely. Moreover, their daily fruit has been manifested to my satisfaction, to be the fruits of that spirit which the *Christians* say, lives in the letters of a book, viz.

Love, peace, joy, long-suffering, gentleness, goodness, faithfulness, meekness, temperance, against which there is no law. Therefore I conclude brother Dooley's text, *Let them alone*, was very pertinent when he came to preach among their neighboring persecutors had he not added, *they be blind leaders of the blind,* etc.

V. It is no matter to me what a tree is called if its fruit is good. If all my neighbors should call my Apple-tree a Buckeye, and tell me that it grew from the seed of Hemlock, this would not alter the taste of the good apple; no more can any name, destroy my regard to a people that bring forth the fruits of righteousness.

But though some may imagine that the name *Shaker* bears analogy to something very mean and [108] contemptible, it has never been my conception of it, nor have I used it at all in that sense.

The first thing that struck me when I heard that name, was that the universal cry in the revival had been that God would *shake the heavens and the earth! Shake out the things that were made, that those things that could not be shaken might remain.* How then was he to do it? He always works by means and instruments.

When the nations were to be threshed, he made Jacob his threshing instrument, of course the men of Jacob were his threshers. People talk of the great wars of Bonaparte, and the great sins that the Devil commits, yet a reasonable person will grant that Bonaparte *wars* with his *warriors,* and the Devil *sins* with his *sinners.* Then was it not reasonable for the subjects of the revival to expect that God would shake the heavens and the earth with his *Shakers?* Some perceiving this tried to substitute his name *Quaker,* but as this name was already appropriated to another people, it only served to take the charge of their first light, and suffer that abuse which the name was originally supposed to merit, until it appeared that the contrast between this people and the *Quak-*

ers in their present standing, rendered it improper to call both by the same name; therefore the general appellation has been finally adopted. *Behold I will send for many fishers, says the Lord, and they shall fish them, and after will I send for many hunters and they shall hunt them from every mountain, etc.* Jer. 16:16. And again, *Saviors shall come up on mount Zion, to judge the mount of Esau and the kingdom shall be the Lord's.* Obadiah, 21. This is a time of universal liberty work, and for each one to be known and distinguished by his works: and has not God a right to work as well as man?, And if he has a work to do with mankind, who can hinder? Therefore, if he sends out many *fishers* to fish them, many *hunters* to hunt them, many, *Shakers* to shake them, and many *Saviors* to save them, let all the people say, Amen. , [109]

[1] The only rule, to direct. See all systems. [105]

[111]
APPENDIX.

Containing a short account of a work of the Good Spirit, among some of the neighboring Indians.
Original pages 111-119

MANY fervent prayers were offered up in the revival for the poor Indians, that they also might share in the blessed hope and joyful anticipation of redeeming love; and missionaries were repeatedly sent out from among the subjects of the work, to convert them to the Christian faith but with little success, as probably they ran like Cushai, before their tidings were ready. From some accounts that were stated by common fame, in the fall of the year 1804, viz. that a great number from different tribes, had met together and held a feast of love and union, danced and rejoiced before the *Great Spirit* and proposed to revive the religion of their ancestors, etc. etc. some were brought to query whether God would not convert the heathen in some way different from what had hitherto been laid out by man: probably move them by his spirit to flow to the church as soon as she was prepared to receive and instruct them, according to Micah iv. 1, 2.

About a year and a half ago, fresh reports broke out concerning them, viz. considerable body of them, had moved down within the boundary line of this state, and were about forming a settlement. Various conjectures were agitated concerning them. Some said they were for war, others, that they were in pursuit of religion and the means of an honest livelihood, were going to work, and in their present circumstances were principally supported by charitable donations from the neighboring whites.

The continuance of these different reports, created an anxiety in the Believers at Turtle-Creek, towards the latter end of last winter, to find out their real situation [112] both in respect to things temporal and spiritual. Accordingly on the 17th of March, 1807, three of the brethren set out in search of them, and on the 23rd of the month arrived at their village. What they discovered on the occasion is briefly comprised in the following extracts of their journal. "When we came in sight of the village the first object that attracted our view was a large frame house, about 150 by 34 feet in size, surrounded with 50 or 60 smoking cottages. We rode up and saluted some men who were standing before the door of a tent, and by a motion of the hand were directed to another wigwam where we found one who could talk English. We asked him if their feelings were friendly.

A. O yes, we are all brothers.

Q. Where are your chiefs, we wish to have talk with them?

A. They are about four miles off, making sugar.

Q. What are their names?

A. Lal-lu-e-tsee-ka, and Te-kum-tha.

Q. Can any of them talk English?

A. No: but there is a good interpreter there, George Blue-jacket. He has gone to school, and can read and talk well.

Q. What Is that big house for?

A. To worship the *Great Spirit.*

Q. How do you worship?

A. Mostly in speaking.

Q. Who is your chief speaker?

A. Our prophet, Lal-lu-e-tsee-ka. He converses with the *Good Spirit,* and tells us how to be good.

Q. Do all that live here, believe in him?

A. Yes we all believe. He can dream to God.

Conducted by a pilot, we repaired to the sugar-camp,

where thirty or forty were assembled with the prophet, who was very sick and confined to his tent. We expressed our desire of having a talk with him. But George informed us that he could not talk to us that ministers of the white people would not believe what he said but counted it foolish and laughed at it, therefore he could not talk; besides he had a pain in his head and [113] was very sick. After informing him that we were not such ministers, he asked:

Do you believe a person can have true knowledge of the *Great Spirit* in the heart, without going to school and learning to read.

A. We believe they can, and that is the best kind of knowledge.

After some talk of this kind with George, he went in to the prophet's tent, where several chiefs were collected, and after continuing their council there about an hour, Lal-lu-e-tsee-ka came out and took his seat in a circle of about 30 persons who sat round the fire. All were silent, every countenance grave and solemn, when he began to speak. His discourse continued about half an hour, in which the most pungent eloquence expressed his deep and heart felt sense of what he spoke, but in language which George said he could not correctly translate into English. However the general sense, he occasionally communicated during our stay.

In the first place, that he (the prophet) had formerly lived on White-river, had been a doctor and a very wicked man. About two years ago, while attending on sick people at Atta-wa, in a time of general sickness, he was struck with a deep and awful sense of his sins, cried mightily to the *Good Spirit* to show him some way of escape, and in his great distress fell into a vision, in which he appeared to be travelling along a road and came to where it forked, the right hand way he was informed led to happiness and the left to misery.

This fork in the road, he was told represented that stage of life in which people were convicted of sin, and those who took the right hand way quit everything that was wicked and became good. But the left hand road was for such as would go on and be bad, after they were shown the right way. They all move slow till they come here, but when they pass the fork to the left, then they go swift. On the left hand way he saw three houses, from the first and second were pathways that led across into the right hand road, but no way leading from the third: This said he, is *Eternity*. He saw vast crowds going swift along the left hand road, and [114] great multitudes in each of the houses, under different degrees of judgment and misery. He mentioned particularly the punishment of the drunkard. One presented him a cup of liquor resembling melted lead, if he refused to drink it he would urge him, saying, come, drink, you used to love whisky. And upon drinking it his bowels were seized with an exquisite burning.

This draught he had often to repeat. At the last house their torment appeared inexpressible, under which he heard them scream, cry pitifully, and roar like the falls of a river. He was afterwards (said the interpreter) taken along the right hand way, which was all interspersed with flowers of delicious smell, and showed a house at the end of it where was everything beautiful, sweet and pleasant, and still went on learning more and more; but in his first vision he saw nothing but the state of the wicked, from which the *Great Spirit* told him to go and warn his people of their danger, and call upon them to put away their sins and be good. Whereupon he began to speak to them in great distress, and would weep and tremble while addressing them. Some believed, were greatly alarmed, began to confess their sins, forsake them, and set out to be good.

This spread the alarm and brought many others from different tribes to see and hear, who were effected in like manner. But some of the chiefs who were very wicked, would not believe, and tried to keep the people from believing, and encouraged them on in their former wicked ways. Whereupon the *Great Spirit* told him to separate from these wicked chiefs and their people, and showed him particularly where to come, towards the big fort where the peace was concluded with the Americans; and there make provisions to receive and instruct all from the different tribes that were willing to be good.

Accordingly all that believed had come and settled there, and a great many Indians had come to hear, and many more were expected. That some white people were afraid, but they were foolish, for they would not hurt any one.

We asked a number of questions: [115]

Q. Do you believe that all mankind are gone away from the *Good Spirit* by wicked works?

A. Yes, that is what we believe: And the prophet feels great pity for all.

Q. Do you believe that the *Good Spirit* once made himself known to the world, by a man that was called Christ?

A. Yes, we believe it, and the *Good Spirit* has showed our prophet what has been in many generations, and he says he wants to talk with some white people about these things.

Q. What sins does your prophet speak most against?

A. Witchcraft, poisoning people, fighting, murdering, drinking whisky, and beating their wives because they will not have children. All such as will not leave off these, go to *Eternity*, He knows all bad people that commit fornication, and can tell it all from seven years old.

Q. What do those do who have been wicked, when they believe the prophet?

A. They confess all.

Q. To whom do they confess?

A. To the prophet and four chiefs.

Q. Do they confess all the bad things they ever did?

A. All from seven years old, And cry and tremble when

they come to confess.

Q. How did you learn this, The Roman Catholics confess their sins?

A. Some *Wiandots* joined the Roman Catholics at Detroit, who now believe in our prophet. Roman Catholics confess their sins but go and do bad again. Our people forsake their bad ways when they have confessed.

They asked us several questions concerning our people, and particularly whether they drank whisky; and appeared not a little rejoiced to learn that there were some among the whites, so far reclaimed, as to lay aside the use of that pernicious liquor. We enquired how they made out for provisions. They answered they had none. So many people came there, eat up all they had raised. [116]

The only meal we saw them eat, was a turkey divided among thirty or forty. And the only relief we could afford them, was ten dollars for the purpose of buying corn.

After the evening conversation closed, we concluded to return to the village with George and several others, and mounted our horses. It was now in the dusk of the evening and the full moon just rising above the horizon, when one of their speakers stood up in an alley between the camps, and spoke for about fifteen minutes with great solemnity, which was heightened at every pause with a loud *seguoy* from the surrounding assembly. On this occasion, our feelings were like Jacob's when he cried out, "*How dreadful is this place! Surely the Lord is in this place!*" And the world know it not. With these impressions we returned to the village and spent the night.

Next morning as soon as it was day, one of their speakers mounted a log near the S. E. corner of the village, and began the morning service with a loud voice, in thanksgiving to the *Great Spirit.* He continued his address for near an hour, The people were all in their tents, some at the distance of fifteen or twenty rods, yet they could all distinctly hear, and gave a solemn and loud assent which sounded from tent to tent, at every pause. While we stood in his view at the end of the meeting house on rising ground, from which we had a prospect of the surrounding wigwams, and the vast open plain or prairie, to the south and east, and which looks over the big fort towards the north, for the distance of two miles, we felt as if we were among the tribes of Israel on their march to Canaan.

Their simplicity and unaffected zeal for the increase of the work of the *Good Spirit*, their ardent desires for the salvation of their unbelieving kindred, with that of all mankind, their willingness to undergo hunger, fatigue, hard labour and sufferings, for the sake of those who came to learn the way of righteousness, and the high expectations they had of multitudes flocking down to hear the prophet the ensuing summer, etc. were considerations truly affecting; while Ske-law-wa hailed the [117] opening day with loud aspirations of gratitude to the *Good Spirit*, and encouraged the obedient followers of divine light to persevere.

They showed us several letters of friendship from the Governor of Ohio, Gen. Whiteman, and others, from which they appeared thankful that the Americans believed their dispositions to be peaceable and brotherly. Their marks of industry were considerable, not only in preparing ground for cultivation, but also in hewing and preparing timber for more commodious buildings. From all we could gather from their account of the work, and of their faith and practice, what we heard and felt in their evening and morning worship, their peaceable disposition and attention to industry, we were induced to believe that God in very deed, was mightily at work among them. And under this impression we invited three or four of them to come down and see us, as soon as they found it convenient.

Near the middle of June, upwards of twenty appeared at Turtle-Creek, encamped in the woods at a small distance from the Church, and tarried four days. They had worship every evening at their encampment, and several on the Sabbath attended the meeting of the *Believers,* and behaved with order and decorum. During their stay, they conducted with peace and civility, and received no contrary treatment from any in the place. And to relieve in some degree, the pressing wants of hungry families at home, twenty-seven horses were loaded back with provision from among the Believers. Yet this act of charity, however small, did not long escape the censorious reflections of some hard-hearted mortals, but even furnished a pretext for implications the most monstrous and unreasonable.

However, in this as in all other cases of the kind, those who busied themselves about what did not concern them, were much divided in their opinion. Some had it, that a number of the Indians had joined the *Shakers,* and many more were coming on: Others, that an Indian had offered to confess his sins, but the *Shakers* could not understand him, and therefore the Indians were convinced too, that the *Shakers* were deceivers. Others [118] tried to make believe that the *Shakers* were encouraging them to war, or at least to contend for the land on which they had settled. And some were foolish enough to go all the way to the village, and put on a mask of hypocrisy to find out from them whether this was not the case. Of all this trouble both of mind and body, such might have been saved had they accustomed themselves at an earlier period, to believe those who tell the truth and nothing but the truth.

About the 12th of August, 1807, they were visited again by two of the brethren from Turtle-Creek, who found them in possession of the same peaceable and brotherly spirit. They had but little conversation with them, yet obtained abundant satisfaction by attending their meeting, which continued from a little after dark till the sun was an hour high the next morning.

The meeting was opened with a lengthy discourse, delivered by the prophet; after which they assembled in a close crowd and continued their worship by singing and shouting that might have been heard, at least to the distance of two miles.

Their various songs and perfect harmony in singing, shouting, etc. rendered the meeting very solemn. But all this appeared far inferior to that solemn fear of God, hatred of sin, and that peace, love and harmony which they manifested among each other. They needed no invitation to pay another visit to Turtle-Creek, nor were they forbidden. Therefore, pursuant to their own choice, a number of them appeared again at the Church, August 29th and were received with usual kindness and charity.

On this occasion some in the neighborhood expressed their uneasiness lest there was some mischievous plot carrying on. But amidst the threats of the ignorant or misinformed, the Shawnees testified that they were wholly for peace, and abundantly proved it by their meekness; gentleness and forbearance. The only expression like resentment that I heard from them on the occasion, was from Nancy, the interpreter, while a bold advocate for the new *Christian* doctrine was boasting how the white people could cut them off; she said, they were for nothing but peace, but if white [119] people would go to war, they would be destroyed by a day of judgment, that not one soul would be left on the face of the earth.

Although these poor Shawnees have had no particular instruction, but what they received by the out-pouring of the spirit, yet in point of real light and understanding, as well as behavior, they shame the Christian world; therefore of that spirit which has wrought in this people so great a change, the Believers at Turtle-Creek are not ashamed; yet they are far from wishing them to turn to the right hand or to the left, to form an external union with them or any other people. But they are willing that God should carry on his work among them without interruption, as he thinks proper.

Lord, what is man! Those great prophets, Marshal, Stone, Thompson, etc. Who were a few years ago crying to sinners to repent, trembling at the view of their danger, searching out and condemning sin, and all the false doctrines invented to palliate [cover, smooth over] it, now building up the same wicked creatures in their sins, and by vain philosophy and a perversion of the sacred scriptures, encouraging them to hope for salvation in some future day; while the trembling Shawnee, obedient to the *Good Spirit* in Lal-lu-e-tsee-ka, Wi-apier-sen-waw, Te-kum-tha and Cum-skaw-kaw, confesses and forsakes his wicked ways, and sets out not merely in a new faith or new doctrine, but *in newness of life and good works.* May not that saying of St. Paul be applicable in such a case: "The heart of this people has waxed, gross, and their ears are dull of hearing, and their eyes have they closed, etc. Therefore be it known, that *the salvation of God* is sent to the Gentiles and they will hear it." [119]

Finished

www.ingramcontent.com/pod-product-compliance
Lightning Source LLC
Chambersburg PA
CBHW020618300426
44113CB00007B/694